SECOND EDITION

BLACK SUNDAY

WHEN WEATHER CLAIMED THE US FIFTH AIR FORCE

MICHAEL JOHN CLARINGBOULD

Black Sunday

When Weather Claimed the US Fifth Air Force

Second Edition

Michael John Claringbould

ISBN: 978-0-6452469-8-8

First published 2022 by Avonmore Books

Avonmore Books

PO Box 217

Kent Town

South Australia 5071

Australia

Phone: (61 8) 8431 9780

avonmorebooks.com.au

NATIONAL LIBRARY OF AUSTRALIA

A catalogue record for this book is available from the National Library of Australia

Cover design & layout by Diane Bricknell

Front Cover Caption: *A Green Dragon Mitchell of the 405th BS leads the way to Saidor as a 13th Bombardment Squadron A-20G and an unidentified Lightning cling to his tail, hoping the pilot knows where he is going. Black Sunday was full of fragmented scenes like this as disoriented aircraft found and then lost others, clinging optimistically in the gloom to anyone who looked like they knew a way home.*

Back Cover Caption: *Captain Morgan Terry and his wingman negotiate wispy stratus over the foothills leading to the Markham Valley. Terry led his flight of five Liberators as low as he dared, flying a new unnamed Liberator. From his rearmost tail gun position, Dick Grills sometimes peered forwards into the fuselage as they came down the valley, seeing the waist gunners "scared to death as we occasionally passed a geographic outcrop".*

CONTENTS

This photograph was taken on 12 September 1996 at RAAF Amberley, Australia, to commemorate the completion of the static restoration of A-20G *The Hell'n Pelican II*. This aircraft had been force-landed in New Guinea by Lieutenant Charles Davidson on Black Sunday, prior to its recovery by the RAAF in 1984. In his commemorative speech Davidson thanked God for his survival. Standing (left to right) are Michael Claringbould, Charles Davidson and Wing Commander Tom Kelly, RAAF, (who had supervised the recovery operation).

MICHAEL CLARINGBOULD – AUTHOR & ILLUSTRATOR

Michael spent his formative years in Papua New Guinea in the 1960s, during which he became fascinated by the many WWII aircraft wrecks which lay around the country and also throughout the Solomon Islands. Michael subsequently served widely overseas as an Australian diplomat throughout Southeast Asia and the Pacific, including Fiji (1995-1998) and Papua New Guinea (2003-2005). Michael has authored and illustrated numerous books on Pacific War aviation. His history of the Tainan Naval Air Group in New Guinea, *Eagles of the Southern Sky*, received worldwide acclaim as the first English-language history of a Japanese fighter unit, and was subsequently translated into Japanese. An executive member of Pacific Air War History Associates, Michael holds a pilot license and PG4 paraglider rating. He continues to develop his skills as a digital aviation artist and illustrator.

OTHER BOOKS BY THE AUTHOR

Eagles of the Southern Sky (2012, with Luca Ruffato)

Nemoto's Travels – The illustrated saga of an IJN floatplane pilot (2021)

Operation I-Go – Yamamoto's Last Offensive – New Guinea & Solomons April 1943 (2020)

Pacific Adversaries Series

Vol One – Japanese Army Air Force vs Allies New Guinea 1942-1944 (2019)

Vol Two – Imperial Japanese Navy vs Allies New Guinea & Solomons 1942-1944 (2020)

Vol Three – Imperial Japanese Navy vs Allies New Guinea & the Solomons 1942-1944 (2020)

Vol Four – Imperial Japanese Navy vs Allies - The Solomons 1943-1944 (2021)

Pacific Profiles Series

Vol One Japanese Army Fighters New Guinea & the Solomons 1942–1944 (2020)

Vol Two Japanese Army Bomber & Other Units, New Guinea & Solomons 1942–44 (2020)

Vol Three Allied Medium Bombers, A-20 Series, South West Pacific 1942–44 (2020)

Vol Four Allied Fighters: Vought F4U Corsair Series Solomons Theatre 1943-1944 (2021)

Vol Five Zero Fighters (land-based) New Guinea & Solomons 1942–1944 (2021)

Vol Six Allied Fighters: Bell Airacobra South & Southwest Pacific 1942–1944 (2022)

Vol Seven Allied Transports: Douglas C-47 South & Southwest Pacific 1942–1945 (2022)

Vol Eight – IJN Floatplanes in the South Pacific 1942–45 (2022)

Vol Nine – Allied Fighters: P-38 series South & Southwest Pacific 1942–1944 (2022)

South Pacific Air War Series (with Peter Ingman)

Volume 1: The Fall of Rabaul December 1941–March 1942 (2017)

Volume 2: The Struggle for Moresby March–April 1942 (2018)

Volume 3: Coral Sea & Aftermath May–June 1942 (2019)

Volume 4: Buna & Milne Bay June–September 1942 (2020)

Volume 5: Crisis in Papua September–December 1942 (2022)

Solomons Air War Series (with Peter Ingman)

Volume 1: Guadalcanal August–September 1942 (2022)

Duel Series (Osprey Publishing)

P-39 / P-400 Airacobra versus A6M2/3 Zero-sen New Guinea 1942 (2018)

F4U Corsair versus A6M2/3/4 Zero-sen, Solomons and Rabaul 1943–44 (2022)

P-47D Thunderbolt versus Ki-43 Hayabusa New Guinea 1943–44 (2020)

A map of New Guinea showing some of the key locations featured in this book. By early 1944 the Fifth Air Force had advanced to northern New Guinea and was utilising bases such as Saidor, Nadzab and Cape Gloucester. Large scale air strikes were waged against key JAAF centres at Wewak and Hollandia, the latter in Dutch New Guinea. The straight-line distance between Nadzab and Hollandia was around 600 miles, but such flights were complicated by the mountainous geography and other factors. By the time of the Black Sunday mission on 16 April 1944, the Fifth Air Force had just begun escorting bombers to Hollandia by making use of the increased endurance of newly delivered P-38J Lightnings.

QUOTES

It was not unusual to walk in mud up to your ankles and it was not uncommon to sneak in at an alternate fighter/bomber strip just before the field was cut off by a tropical storm. King weather was a troublemaker.

LIGHTNING PILOT CARROLL ANDERSON

THE 43RD BG OFFICIAL HISTORY

Weather which had been bearable on the way up, became unbearable on the return. The searchlights of Nadzab stayed on very late. Their long blue fingers hung motionless against the sky, hopeful beacons to guide home aircraft that we all knew were long since down somewhere in the jungle or the sea. Elaborate precautions had always been taken to guard against a catastrophe like this, but apparently our efforts haven't been good enough. Mark Twain would have been nonplussed to see how the men of the Fifth Air Force went after the problem which he said everyone talked about, but nobody ever did anything to solve . . .

There were lots of ways to get killed in the Southwest Pacific and weather was one of our worst hazards.

LIGHTNING PILOT LEROY ROSS

GLOSSARY & ABBREVIATIONS

Japanese terms are in italics. All Japanese names are presented in the traditional way of writing Japanese, with the surname presented first.

AA	Anti-Aircraft
ADVON	Advanced Echelon of the Fifth Air Force. Essentially this comprised all combat units on frontline airfields.
Air Apaches	345th Bombardment Group
ASI	Air Speed Indicator
BG	Bombardment Group
Blackcat	callsign for a USN PBY
BS	Bombardment Squadron
Chutai	An aircraft formation which normally comprised a strength of nine aircraft. JAAF fighter units normally had three *chutai*, Nos. 1, 2 and 3, plus a headquarters detachment.
Chutaicho	A flight leader of officer rank who commands a JAAF *chutai*.
CMS	Combat Mapping Squadron
CO	Commanding Officer
CRTC	Combat Replacement Training Center
FG	Fighter Group
Flying Circus	380th Bombardment Group
FS	Fighter Squadron
Grim Reapers	3rd Bombardment Group
Guinea Short Lines	25th Liaison Squadron
Hayabusa	Peregrine Falcon (JAAF name for Ki-43 "Oscar" fighter)
Hien	Flying Swallow (JAAF name for Ki-61 "Tony" fighter)
HMAS	His Majesty's Australian Ship
IJN	Imperial Japanese Navy
JAAF	Japanese Army Air Force
Jolly Rogers	90th Bombardment Group

Ken's Men	43rd Bombardment Group
LCT	Landing Craft, Tank
LST	Landing Ship, Tank
MIA	Missing in Action
mph	miles per hour
NFS	Night Fighter Squadron
POW	Prisoner of War
PRG	Photographic Reconnaissance Group
PRS	Photographic Reconnaissance Squadron
PSP	Pierced Steel Planking
PT boat	Patrol Torpedo boat
RAAF	Royal Australian Air Force
RAN	Royal Australian Navy
Red Raiders	22nd Bombardment Group
Roarin' 20s	312th Bombardment Group
RPM	Revolutions per Minute
Satan's Angels	475th Fighter Group
Sky Lancers	417th Bombardment Group
Sun Setters	38th Bombardment Group
SWPA	South West Pacific Area
TRG	Tactical Reconnaissance Group
TRS	Tactical Reconnaissance Squadron
US	United States
USN	United States Navy
USAAF	United States Army Air Force

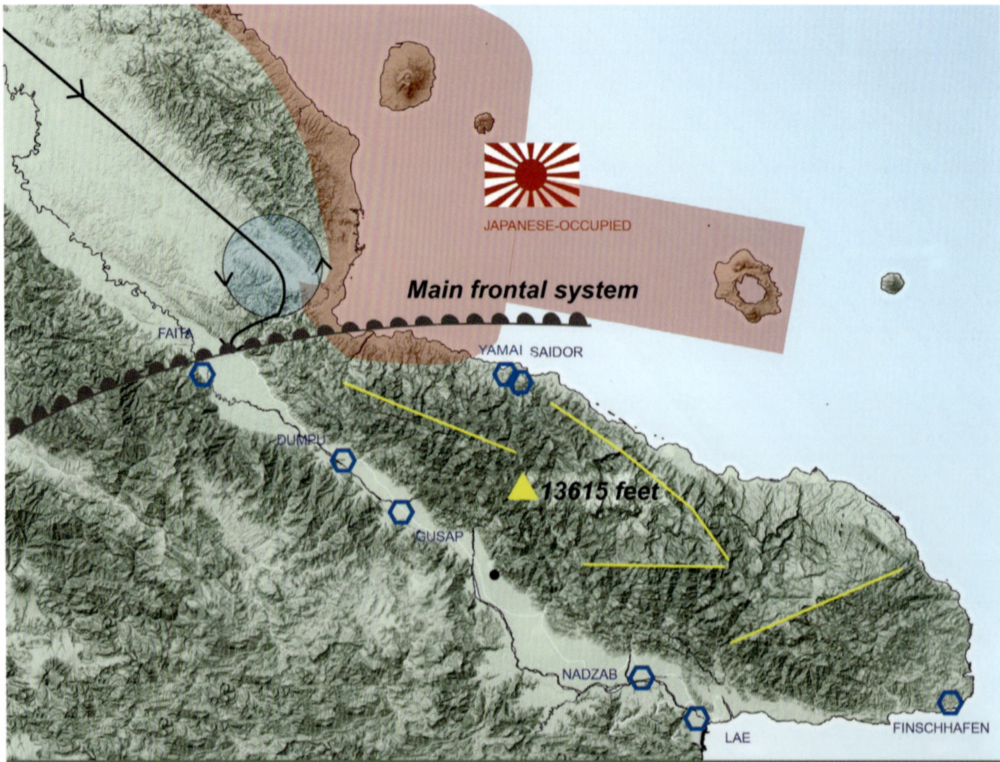

The blue hexagons in this map represent Allied bases and airfields. Most of the airpower involved in the Black Sunday mission had departed from two bases in the Markham Valley, Gusap and Nadzab. While the valley had flat areas suitable for airfields, it was hemmed in by mountains on each side. To the north, the Finesterre Ranges towered to almost 14,000 feet. The highest point in the Finesterres is marked with a yellow triangle while other main mountain spines are shown with yellow lines.

On the way back from their mission over Hollandia on Black Sunday 16 April 1944, the attackers route back into the Markham Valley was blocked by a massive weather front as shown. The light blue circle is where many circled, mostly counter clockwise, trying to find a gap in the weather to enable them to enter the Markham Valley.

As aircraft began to run low on fuel, the options of baling out, ditching in the ocean or force landing in a grass clearing were complicated by the proximity of Japanese forces, as shown.

PREFACE

The day of Sunday 16 April 1944 marks the biggest non-combat loss the USAAF incurred in any theatre in World War II. After a delayed morning departure more than three hundred Fifth Air Force aircraft departed to attack Japanese airfields and installations at Hollandia in Dutch New Guinea. Not one aircraft was lost to enemy action, but over three dozen were lost to a vicious weather front. The date quickly became known as Black Sunday within the Fifth Air Force.

With the benefit of hindsight, we can see that the mission was superfluous and made minimal difference to the subsequent US landing at Hollandia. However, US commanders were not to know this at the time and the mission proceeded much because it had been set in stone. The timing of it was not, however, and it still unclear why it was authorised at such late notice when the forecast mitigated so strongly against this decision.

While the crews carried out their mission, a massive frontal system blocked off safe return. That late afternoon no part of New Guinea's sky was still and as aircraft scurried everywhere each loss was directly attributable to the powerful forces of nature which dominated all outcomes. Dirty weather scored a clean kill over many, making mockery of the carefully planned strike.

There is considerable irony in the fact that the mission, incurring the Fifth Air Force's biggest loss, occurred when it was at its greatest strength in New Guinea. It had grown exponentially since the first USAAF involvement in the theatre, a B-17 raid against Rabaul on 23 January 1942. This led to a situation in April 1944 whereby the Markham Valley bases heaved with US air power, to the extent that several RAAF squadrons were asked to vacate Nadzab to make way for yet more incoming units. Subsequent to Black Sunday, strikes in New Guinea were wound back, while combat units focussed on moving to Hollandia as soon as possible, and thus vacating the New Guinea theatre.

Recounting chronologically the day's events is impossible due to the resultant chronological chaos. The line between survivors and victims was fine, and fates fell either way for no apparent reason. The intensity of each personal experience meant that each individual perspective was narrow. A compilation of the day's rich history reveals a fast-moving, unstoppable tragedy in which luck played more than a leading role.

It is less complicated to write of success - an enemy routed and a plan fulfilled. Black Sunday is the antithesis of such an event. The day and its aftermath epitomise the type of war which the Fifth Air Force came to know so well.

INTRODUCTION TO SECOND EDITION

I am pleased to present an updated version of a book I first started researching in 1990 when I discovered that the biggest weather-related loss in aviation history had slipped quietly into a half-century void. Whilst the individual units involved recorded the day's events as they pertained to them, no overview had ever been compiled. So, in the end I wrote the account because no-one else had.

The genesis of this book can be traced to a composite list of aircraft lost that fateful day, provided by Bruce Hoy[1] when I visited his Brisbane home in 1990. Afterwards I received information from many quarters, including dozens of mission veterans, then still alive and happy to recount their experiences. The text for the first edition was drafted in 1991 at Bang Seray, Thailand, whilst I took respite from my duties at the Australian Embassy in Bangkok. Since publishing the first edition in 2000 I continued to collect further photos and material. This expanded and updated edition incorporates considerable new material, including rare photos. Digital graphics enable us to see accurate replicas of the participant aircraft. Assembling the logistics of the mission constituted a complicated jigsaw, down to identifications of individual aircraft and crews.

I avoided passing judgement or making assumptions in the narrative; it is unfair to judge any event by contemporary standards. Aviation and navigation technology of the time was basic by today's standards. Continuous reference to units and aircraft by military terminology is hard to avoid. A minimum amount of such references, tedious as they will doubtless be to many, are unavoidable to make sense of the day's complex movements.

I was made privy to a collection of personal letters written by the families of those who lost loved ones to Black Sunday. In the interests of privacy, I have published none of these. Of this and related material I will say however that the extent to which truth inevitably surfaces fifty years later surprised me. Since the first edition several MIA cases have been resolved. All save one appear straightforward cases of having been swallowed by the storm or captured by the Japanese.

That exception continues to be the crew of 387th BS A-20G *The Texan*, Captain Frank Smart and gunner Sergeant Mike Music. On this matter I overturned every clue including relevant captured Japanese diaries. Japanese units in around Saidor were scattered, emaciated and undisciplined. Unless direct confrontation arose, they had no reason to harass two Allied airmen so close to a US base. Perhaps both men lost their weapons in the ditching, or they were rendered unserviceable. Perhaps they drowned while trying to cross a flooded river or stream, of which several were in the area. Nonetheless, their

1 Bruce Hoy was employed as the Director of the Papua New Guinea National Museum in the 1980s.

disappearance portends an obscurity as perplexing now as it was then. With so many parties focused on their rescue, their homecoming was a reliable assumption. I can offer no satisfactory explanation, their fate all the more tragic for a disappearance in a remote land which bore them no witness.

I hope you enjoy reading *Black Sunday* as much as I enjoyed researching it.

Michael John Claringbould
Canberra, Australia
March 2022

Taken on the actual morning of the mission at Nadzab, a crew chief straps Lieutenant Bob Tomberg into his 433rd FS P-38J #177, as he is about to embark on his 100th mission. The availability of the new "J" model Lightnings with their improved range enabled bombers to be escorted during raids on distant Hollandia.

CHAPTER 1

TARGET HOLLANDIA

By March 1944 Allied planning in the SWPA focused on the neutralisation of Hollandia and nearby areas. The strategy, initiated by General Douglas MacArthur, was intended to by-pass and isolate General Adachi Hatazo's Imperial Japanese 18th Army entrenched at Wewak. MacArthur wanted Hollandia in Allied hands by late April, and once achieved, Allied forces would be placed to consolidate New Guinea operations before invading the Philippines. The final blueprint for the invasion and occupation of Hollandia, code-named Operation *Reckless*, had been approved at MacArthur's headquarters in Brisbane, Australia, on 25 March 1944. Despite initial conviviality at the meeting, MacArthur and the US Navy Pacific commander, Admiral Chester Nimitz, had differed over the risk posed by remaining Japanese airpower. In concluding, Nimitz refused to send his carriers into the waters off Hollandia, arguing that the enemy still retained potent regional air forces. For his part, the commander of the USAAF Fifth Air Force, Lieutenant General George Kenney, persuaded MacArthur that his Fifth Air Force could eliminate enemy air power on the ground. Kenney even set the deadline of 5 April by which to achieve this. MacArthur had faith in Kenney's abilities thus gave him the green light. Kenney then returned to Port Moresby to prepare his air force.

The Hollandia base area, near Tanahmerah Bay in Dutch New Guinea, included three Japanese inland airfield complexes: Sentani, Cyclops, and Hollandia. Vast quantities of supplies were dispersed and stockpiled along the northern shoreline from Jangena to Depapre villages, and around the villages of Tablasoeta, Pim and Mariboe. More were hidden under the palms of Stuber's Plantation. The area was scenic; immediately south of the town was Lake Sentani, a placid freshwater lake some fifteen miles long, surrounded by rolling grass plains.

In New Guinea, the moral question of attacking native villages in enemy held areas had proved problematic. It was appreciated that unwarranted attacks on defenceless friendly natives would alienate them, making it less safe for downed airmen in that particular area. However, the Japanese deliberately used native villages to store materiel, recognising the Allied reluctance to attack them. The Fifth Air Force had developed a policy that only localities known to be occupied by the enemy would be attacked. All villages around Hollandia were considered enemy occupied.

Japanese forces operated two air forces under the separate jurisdiction of the Army and Navy, with no naval aerial units based at Hollandia. However, the Japanese 4th Air Army had despatched hundreds of reinforcement aircraft to Hollandia in the preceding weeks. A paucity of earth revetments offered limited protection, however, and most aircraft had to be parked in the open. Japanese movements were largely known due to the interception and decoding of Japanese transmissions. A particularly important message was picked up on the late afternoon of 29 March, a message which would expedite Operation *Reckless.* The encoded text was immediately passed to MacArthur's rear headquarters in Brisbane, delivered that evening by Australian 1st Wireless Unit member Frank Patrick directly to MacArthur's chief signals officer, Major General Spencer Akin. Spencer answered the door in pyjamas, but rallied to let the messenger in. After reading the message, he was on the lift to Kenney's room upstairs. Akin described the situation:

> An important intercept from Japanese High Command to the commander of the Japanese Air Force at the Hollandia air base was brought to me in my room in Brisbane. It directed the Japanese Hollandia commander to evacuate all of his airplanes from Hollandia as early as practical the next morning as it was expected that Allied bombers would soon attack that base. I immediately took the message to General Kenney who then immediately sent an order to his air commander in New Guinea, General Ennis Whitehead, directing that he have the Hollandia air base attacked before the enemy could evacuate.

The Allied frontline airfields centred around Nadzab and Gusap in the Markham Valley were far from Hollandia, however. Although Japanese commanders assessed correctly that the Fifth Air Force would not send medium bombers on long-range missions without fighter protection, the pace and intensity of the Allied advance clearly had made them cautious. They calculated that Hollandia remained outside the range of the Fifth's fighters, however this was not the case. Recent factory modifications by Lockheed to their successful P-38 Lightning had produced the "J" model, a variant with improved range. In addition, many of the Fifth's older P-38 "F" and "G" variants had since been field-modified with additional fuel tanks. When the Fifth received its first P-38Js this ability of additional range had been kept quiet. Squadron commanders had ordered their pilots not to proceed beyond Tadji with "J" models, even under duress of combat.

At Nadzab both the 475th and 8th FGs harboured a suite of new and shiny natural metal finish P-38J-15s which had been assembled at Eagle Farm outside Brisbane. In preparation for the Hollandia strikes, several pilots on leave in Sydney had been pulled from leave without notice to deliver these new mounts. The delivery route was via Townsville, where they were refuelled before the final direct leg to Nadzab which took them over the Owen Stanley Ranges without stopping at Port Moresby. Older former camouflaged models were then redistributed among other fighter squadrons. Whilst most of these coveted fighters went to the 475th FG, the 80th FS had also received a handful of P-38J-15s for the job. Their older "H" models meanwhile went to the 36th FS.

Air Strikes Commence

Whilst the USAAF had been bombing Hollandia occasionally since 8 March 1944, the intercept which had created so much fuss in Brisbane caused the first major Hollandia strike to proceed on 30 March 1944 at short notice indeed, conducted by Liberators. It went well, with no losses and most bombs on target. The Japanese had initially been taken by surprise: the Australian 1st Wireless Unit intercepted Hollandia's air raid warning sent only eighteen minutes before the first raid. But a repeat raid by heavies the next day of 31 March triggered a response of an estimated 50 enemy fighters, which had been given a good 70 minutes warning to get airborne.

A 43rd BG B-24J flies over the wide Ramu Valley with the Markham River in view below left. Liberators had been bombing Hollandia since early March 1944, but flew the first major strike on 30 March 1944.

Whilst the estimate of 50 fighters was a gross exaggeration, even more so were the claimed kills by the covering 80th and 431st FS Lightnings which were awarded fourteen fighters against a true score of none shot down. Nonetheless by mid-February 1944 the JAAF in New Guinea had reached a desperate phase. The entire JAAF fighter contingent around Wewak by month's end comprised only eight *Hayabusa* and six *Hien*. They staged a dawn attack against Nadzab on 13 February with a motley collection of 59th, 63rd and 248th *Sentai Hayabusa*, however by early March the 63rd *Sentai* was down to just a handful of fighters. On 9 March it could only rally one airborne at 2134 to intercept an incoming threat. In late March this regiment retreated to Hollandia, from where it flew its last mission on 21 April 1944.

Both the 33rd and 77th *Sentai* were sent to Hollandia in late February 1944 from Southeast Asia to bolster the fraught situation. Once they reached Hollandia it was decided to send them further east to reinforce Wewak's feeble fighter strength so both units, operating together, redeployed there on 26 February into Wewak's damaged airfields. There, all of the *sentai* were placed under the command of the 14th Air Brigade and paired as "Air Attack" units: the pairings were the 68th and 78th *Sentai* (*Hien* outfits but mainly operating

Hayabusa), the 63rd and 248th *Sentai* (*Hayabusa*), and the 33rd and 77th *Sentai* (*Hayabusa*). On morning of 11 March at Wewak, with the 33rd *Sentai* reduced to eighteen fighters, all were ordered to return to Hollandia to harbour them from further US air attack. Then, by end of March 1944 the feared Ki-61 Tony fighter had all but disappeared from New Guinea skies. On 6 March 78th *Sentai* pilot Lieutenant Asai Mitsuada was lost, and this was the last Tony lost in New Guinea.

From the first two days of the Hollandia bombing campaign ADVON claimed 138 enemy aircraft destroyed on the ground. Signals interception indicated the Japanese intention to evacuate the remaining aircraft by moving them westward to Noemfoor, Biak or as far away as Ambon. This was challenging however as these bases lacked facilities to receive large numbers of aircraft, and bomb craters which the Fifth's heavies had placed in Hollandia's runways made departure difficult. Then, whilst the Japanese were in the midst of confusion and also short of anti-aircraft ammunition, the Fifth's assault on Hollandia recommenced. Four further large-scale co-ordinated strikes were flown or attempted on 3, 5, 8 and 12 April 1944, this time with combined force of heavy, medium and light bombers escorted by the new Lightnings.

The 3 April 1944 mission was the last in which there was substantial fighter resistance over Hollandia. As both sides traded blows, Lieutenant Joe Barton and his Lightning were lost to Japanese fighters. In return the Lightnings claimed 25 Japanese Oscars, however only two were shot down, both from the 33rd *Sentai*. After this raid Hollandia's airpower was no longer considered a threat, and this was largely understood by Allied intelligence.

Nonetheless, Macarthur wanted more strikes to be sure. On the 5 April mission a *Flying Circus* Liberator presented a grisly spectacle when its Number Four engine faltered on take-off from Nadzab. With a full fuel and bomb load the bomber spun into the ground. Then on the return from the target, a *Roarin' 20s* A-20G lost power in both engines due to incorrect fuel management. The aircraft descended smoothly before exploding into foothills below.

Cloud cover turned back the Mitchells and A-20Gs on the 8 April mission. In the tightly turning formations there was a lucky reprieve after one *Roarin' 20* had its tail chewed by another. Both returned safely to Gusap, although their pilots came close to blows after landing. At higher altitude, the Liberators meanwhile broke through the cloud to to deliver their bombs.

An intercepted message from the Japanese 1st Air Route Unit on 9 April 1944 advised that only 2,630 gallons of aircraft fuel remained at Hollandia. Nonetheless, aircraft were still using Hollandia's runways. Two days later the commanding officer of the Japanese 6th Air Division, Lieutenant General Itahana Gi'ichi, flew to Hollandia to for an emergency meeting to evaluate the rapidly deteriorating situation.

The 12 April mission produced a mystery when an 822nd BS B-25G forced-landed in the Sepik Delta on its return. Its crew were seen waving from the intact aircraft, but then disappeared. It turned out that Lieutenant Math English and all of the crew were executed

An abandoned 33rd *Sentai* Oscar is found by US troops at Cape Gloucester. By the time of the Black Sunday mission JAAF aerial resistance had all but disappeared.

by the Japanese after they walked into the village of Paiambit. Meanwhile this strike focused on Hollandia township instead of the airfields but was marred by the systematic destruction of Liberator *Yankee Doodle Dandy*. Attacked by mottled green 33rd *Sentai* Oscars, they conducted only hesitating attacks until the Liberator fell back and became easy prey. The fighters forced it to crash into a 6,000-foot mountain southwest of Hollandia. From this aerial combat the Fifth's top-scoring ace Richard Bong claimed three of the nine awarded Oscars, and the commanding officer of the 80th FS, Captain Jay Robbins, two. In fact, only three were shot down during the entire engagement, two from the 77th *Sentai* and 68th *Sentai chutaicho* Captain Takenawa Toshio who successfully baled out.

This series of missions, in reality unexceptional by Fifth Air Force standards, nevertheless achieved Kenney's promise of the wholesale destruction of Japanese air power at Hollandia. Prior to the seaborne invasion of the area, only a week or so away, one final raid was planned. The mission was set for 16 April, the first Sunday after Easter.

The Lurking Front

The Fifth's meteorological facilities were deployed in good faith. Right up until the evening before the strike, ADVON's meteorological officers remained wary of a frontal system which was building over the Bismarck Sea. Squalls and low cloud led to cancelled strikes against Tadji on 14 April, however they proceeded the following day. Logistical planning for Operation *Reckless* was advanced by now, however, and pressure was on to deliver the last blow on schedule. On Saturday evening 15 April, two 43rd BG Liberators were despatched from Nadzab to conduct overnight weather reconnaissance of New Guinea's northern coastline as far as Tadji. Returning early on the morning of the strike,

An A-20G strafes its way across one of Hollandia's airfields during the 3 April 1944 raid.

they reported by radio widespread cloud over the target, before ominously diverting, one to Saidor and the other to Finschhafen.

Early on Sunday morning 16 April four 421st NFS Lightnings conducted an early morning tactical strike mission along the northern coastline. Departing at 0625, they returned mid-morning to report the weather flyable. However, the most comprehensive weather reconnaissance was conducted by Captain George Flannery and Lieutenant Robert Toothman, pilots attached to Fifth Bomber Command Headquarters which had a special unit tasked especially for weather-snooper missions. Two days prior to Black Sunday, Toothman had mapped out the mission's departure route, rendezvous points, procedures and timings from Nadzab. The unit was currently operating late-model B-25Gs as they had marginally better performance than the older "D" models. These weather reconnaissances were not without risk. Only three weeks prior one of this unit's B-25Gs had disappeared over the northern New Guinea coast around Madang. Its burned-out wreckage was subsequently discovered by Boomerangs of No. 4 Squadron, RAAF, on 18 April, while searching for Black Sunday survivors.

Early on Black Sunday's morning Toothman and Flannery proceeded separately as far as Tadji, each with two weather observers aboard who issued weather reports to Bomber Command every thirty minutes. Importantly, Toothman also had the authority to attach pilot recommendations about the weather:

> I did so, saying it was terrible. I was astounded when at the head of the Markham Valley around Gusap flying about 500 feet above the valley and under full overcast we ran into B-24s, B-25s, then the A-20s and P-38s. I called to Sergeant Moell, my radioman, and asked him to recheck the "Roger" on our transmissions to Bomber Command. I thought to myself that there would be hell to pay today and when I got back to the base I went to the intelligence people to confirm our bad WX reports.

When he landed back at Nadzab, Toothman confirmed that Flannery, as commander of the weather unit, had also recommended that the mission be cancelled. The unit's "Weather Central" building was built on a small hill to the north of Nadzab, overlooking the base where Sergeant Jay Morgan supervised and coordinated all incoming reports. Despite these adverse reports and negative recommendations, ADVON overrode them and authorised the strike. The only proviso was that take-off could be delayed, as required, to allow cloud and overcast to dissipate. Ironically the resultant decision to delay departure would be ultimately responsible for the losses about to ensue.

Unbeknownst to planners and pilots alike, aeronautical charts pertaining to the Finesterre Ranges contained inaccurate topographical information, the highest point of which is 13,615 feet. Most wartime maps had the highest point at only 9,100 feet! Critically, no strafer crews carried maps except squadron leaders. Especially for the mediums, the A-20Gs and B-25s, fuel became the most critical factor, but especially the former type whose fuel gauges strained on every Hollandia mission. The disproportionate number of A-20Gs claimed on the day reflected this.

(Left to Right) Captains Art Peregoy and John Ehlinger of the 475th FG, along with Captain George Morgan, weather officer Sergeant Jay Morgan (circled and no relation) and Captain William Anderson of the 39th FS at Nadzab's "Weather Central" a few days after Black Sunday (a "Weather Central" sign is just visible behind the vehicle). These pilots were visiting Sergeant Morgan for a briefing on forecasting services.

Journey to Hollandia

Diversions along the attack route were neither expected nor planned, with Wewak nominated as an alternate target if the force could not get through. As on previous Hollandia missions, participants would fly northwest inland, almost paralleling New Guinea's northern coastline, with a mid-way checkpoint at Burui village, easily found as it lay on the shore of Lake Chambri. For those based at Nadzab and Gusap, the return journey brought them back through the Ramu and Markham Valleys to airfields wedged between the dominating Finesterre and Bismarck Ranges. In fine weather, returning aircrews could see New Guinea's highest mountain to their right - the greenish-purple relief of Mount Wilhelm reaching 14,793 feet. On the other side, the Finesterre Ranges projected a sharp and purplish jagged outline, some peaks reaching almost as high. Prior to entering the Ramu Valley from the north are the low foothills behind Madang. In April 1944 these were pervaded by desperate Japanese soldiers, retreating towards Wewak under constant pressure from combined Allied air attack in conjunction with Australian ground forces.

Options for downed aircrews were limited in a harsh environment of either jungle or swamp. If forced to land anywhere other than at an Allied airfield or baling out the chance of enemy capture was high. Parachuting into jungle (and thus high trees) carried a high chance of breaking bones or being knocked unconscious. The broad coastal Sepik Plain contains fetid swamps, fit only for insects, disease and carnivores. The Finesterre Ranges, unless following streams or isolated native tracks, remain impassable to this day. A 3rd Australian Division despatch dated August 1943, describes the area:

> … such conditions of rain, mud, rottenness, stench, and above all, the feeling of being shut in by everlasting jungle and ever-ascending mountains, are sufficient to fray the strongest nerves.

An unidentified Japanese officer of the 115th Regiment agreed:

> One advances as in the dark. No matter to what place one climbs, the eye can penetrate only a short distance, and since one cannot depend on this to see the form of the mountains in the vicinity, it is difficult to orientate the actual terrain with maps.

On early Saturday evening before the attack Catholic and Protestant Masses were held at Gusap. The aircrews prepared for a dawn departure similar to the previous Hollandia missions, but cloud and rain delayed departure. As a result, the first engine cranked three hours late.

CHAPTER 2

THE COMBINED FORCE

Four main aircraft types would form the attacking force:

- 59 Liberators from the 22nd (*Red Raiders*), 43rd (*Ken's Men*) and 90th (*Jolly Rogers*) Heavy Bombardment Groups
- 51 Mitchells from the 38th *Sunsetter* and 345th *Air Apache* BGs
- 87 A-20Gs from the 3rd Bombardment Group *Grim Reapers* and the 312th and 417th *Sky Lancer* Light Bombardment Groups.
- The total fighter force comprised 80 Lightnings from the 475th and 8th Fighter Groups. This escort force was originally intended to include three squadrons from the 35th FG totalling 48 P-47D Thunderbolts to greet and escort home incoming bombers, however in the end all three squadrons aborted when recalled by 19th Sector Fighter Control due to the weather, or decisions by the squadron commanders.

Assigned to conduct photographic reconnaissance of both the Hollandia and Tadji areas before and after the strike were six 20th Combat Mapping Squadron F-7As (converted Liberators), along with a mixture of six F-5As and two F-5Bs (converted Lightnings) from the 8th, 25th and 26th PRS. Separately Blackcat PBY-5 Catalinas from VP-34 were strategically moving to various locations including Saidor and Langemak Bay near Finschhafen to rescue crews who might ditch or need offshore rescue. These included Lieutenant Norman Paxton flying PBY #72 in the vicinity of Manum Island and Lieutenant (jg) Nathan Gordon in #61.

Both the F-5 reconnaissance Lightning and F-7A reconnaissance Liberator entered the theatre painted blue for high altitude camouflage. The Japanese had quickly come to realise that any blue aircraft played a reconnaissance role. In addition, the blue paint reduced the F-5's cruise speed by ten miles per hour. The distinctive colour of both types thus ear-marked targets of Allied interest to the Japanese. Accordingly, by April 1944 units which operated reconnaissance Lightnings were in the process of paint-stripping their mounts down to natural metal finish. The F-7As would soon follow.

The 20th CMS F-7As had deployed to New Guinea in April 1944 as the first multi-engine reconnaissance unit assigned to the Fifth Air Force. The F-7As were Liberator airframes, factory-converted in Minnesota by removing the bomb racks and adding two fuel tanks in the forward bomb bay. The aft bomb bay was also converted into a photo bay with mounts and windows for two vertical reconnaissance cameras, mostly 9 x 18-inch format K-18 cameras with f6.0 lenses of 24-inch focal length. Three suites of mapping cameras

The colourful artwork on F-7A reconnaissance Liberator *Little Joe.* During the Black Sunday mission Major Joe Davis led the six 20th CMS F-7As from Nadzab in this aircraft.

comprised 9 x 9-inch negative K-17 cameras with high resolution metrogon lenses in a tri-metrogon array, mounted in the nose to provide horizon-to-horizon coverage. Six were required on this mission as extensive photographic coverage of the coastline was required to plan the amphibious invasion planned for 22 April.

This squadron would depart Nadzab at 1000. The previous evening just before midnight squadron Operations Officer Captain Jim Adams briefed crews that their photographic coverage of the target would be used to plan the invasion. That evening Adams stressed probable frontal activity, indicating Saidor as an emergency alternative landing ground. Further away, the strip at Cape Gloucester on the island of New Britain was also earmarked.

Other limited strikes were scheduled for targets along the northern coast, comprising barge-hunting missions from Uligan Harbour to Bogia. These would be flown by 82nd and 110th TRS Airacobras, separate from the main strike force. On Black Sunday then, the Fifth was about to launch more than three hundred aircraft, their biggest effort in the theatre to date. More than 1,300 aircrew would fly the mission.

Positioned in the wide Markham Valley, Nadzab's five bitumen interconnected runways were supplemented by eighteen square miles of ammunition dumps, encampments and roads. Most participants would depart from here, along with other units departing from Gusap and Saidor. The coordinated strike required staggered departure times for the different groups to accommodate different cruising speeds and distances from separate bases. It took time to taxi and assemble airborne squadrons, however, and the revised departure time, thus incurring related adjustments, further complicated synchronising the raid. The planned order of attack was Liberators first at high altitude, followed by Mitchells at medium altitudes, then strafing A-20Gs last, all escorted by Lightnings. The reconnaissance photo-ships would photograph the results from high above before and after the last bombs struck. This was the plan, which all things considered, commenced satisfactorily.

Departure Delayed

A bleak Sunday morning dawned, blanketed by thick low overcast. Heavy rain had fallen most of the night, and the sky remained heavy, cloudy and damp. After making their way to mess shacks for breakfast, crews at all departure bases sipped coffee, and ate their way through pancakes and fried eggs. Few discussed the forthcoming mission. Old hands reasoned that the danger posed by this particular Hollandia mission was less than previous ones. Since the last Hollandia raid four days ago on 12 April, daily missions to the Tadji and Hansa Bay areas had encountered no enemy fighters. Intelligence assessments predicted no fighter interception unless reinforcements had arrived. Given the recent damage to Hollandia's runways and taxiways, this was unlikely. The assessment turned out to be correct.

The Liberators

With an initial forecast for clearing weather, the *Jolly Rogers*' group Intelligence Officer cut orders for the group's Liberators to commence departure at 0825. In the event the first Black Sunday aircraft to depart, five 320th BS Liberators, launched at 0900. Followed by the 400th BS, the remaining two *Jolly Rogers* squadrons, the 321st and 319th, were both airborne by 0935. This group was the longest-serving Liberator outfit in the Fifth Air Force and was still operating "D" model Liberators whilst more recent Liberator outfits enjoyed the newer "J" models. At this stage of the war each *Jolly Roger* wore a large stencilled white grinning skull and crossbones on its fins, the group's landmark marking. Among the *Jolly Rogers*' Liberators were *Kay-O, Heaven Can Wait, Big Chief, Ready, Willing & Able, Louisiana Lullaby, The Powers Girl, Sad Sack, Sky Witch, Shamrock Sherry, Upstairs Maid, Snappin'N a Bitin'* and *Betsy.*

Four squadrons of *Red Raider* Liberators next lined up and departed Nadzab at 45-second intervals. In their midst many featured colourful nose-art including *Marie, Titian Temptress, Sweet Takeoff, Queen Anne, Kansas City Kitty, Miss Leading* (Lieutenant Edward Halper), *Shoo Shoo Baby, Our Honey, Tabu, Island Queen, The Lemon* (Lieutenant John Hellstrom), *Our Gal III* (Lieutenant Louis Perraud), *Sweet Raquot* (Lieutenant LM Wiggins), *Lost Angel* (Lieutenant Dwain Harry) and *Sandy* (Lieutenant HA Dunn). Likewise, *Ken's Men* Liberators also displayed fine artwork including *Ace Of Spades, Lady Luck, Miss Liberty, King Of Clubs, Mallet Head, Queen Of Hearts, At Ease, The Mayflower, Mag The Hag, Lucky Lucille, Shirley Anne, Two Bob Tillie, Kentucky Virgin, Joltin' Janie II, Rio Rita, Satan's Sister, Whistle Stop* and *Gentleman Jim.*

At the other end of the scale in size, two small Gusap-based No. 4 Squadron (RAAF) Boomerang reconnaissance fighters, A46-148 and A46-119, departed Gusap to undertake reconnaissance of retreating pockets of Japanese troops around Bogadjim at 1030. Both returned early at 1315 due to low cloud. This unit would soon be involved in searches for downed US airmen.

The Mitchells

For *Air Apache* Mitchell crews, their briefing took place in individual squadron headquarters shacks alongside Nadzab airfields Three and Four. For the 345th BG, which usually flew strafing missions, this mission was a change of pace: along with 38th BG Mitchells they would release their bombs from medium altitude. By now Hollandia was familiar to them, and the crews anticipated another long and tedious flight to target. Little emphasis was placed on the weather, except to note that take-off might be delayed. Following their briefing crews from the 499th, 500th and 501st BS (the 498th BS was rostered off) made their way to the flight lines. Although take-off time at this stage remained uncertain, crew chiefs got to work. Engines were checked and warmed, and the more staccato tone of the Wright radial engines contrasted with the humming of the in-line Allison engines installed in the Lightnings in distant hardstands. Occasionally a gripe was made about the delay. Then word came down. The Wrights cranked again, this time for real, and the first *Air Apache* launched at 1015.

All these three squadrons would bomb independently, each structured into arrowhead formations of three flights of three. After departure the three squadrons formed up alongside the 38th BG's four squadrons over the Lerone River, before joining their Lightning escort overhead Burui. All seven Mitchell squadrons cruised to the target area at 8,000 feet, with each aircraft loaded with 260-pound canisters of parafrags.[1]

The 500th BS's nine Mitchells led the *Air Apaches* and were commanded by Lieutenant Dale Speicher from an unnamed Mitchell. This squadron was tasked to bomb supply areas from 6,500 feet along the road from Jautefa Bay to Hollandia's three airfields. *Pannell Job* turned back shortly after reaching Burui with fuel transfer problems, whilst *Rita's Wagon, Bachelor Made, WAC-a-Teer Off Duty, Fitch's Bitch, Skippy* and three other unnamed bombers continued. Nine 499th BS Mitchells were led by Captain Richard Baker from a brand-new unnamed B-25D-30. This squadron was tasked to focus on a square 500 x 500 yards off the road leading to Pim village. Most Mitchells had names; Baker was accompanied by *Hardstand Hattie, Generator, Slapsy, Hell's Belles, Uneager Beaver, L'il Shiftless, Stingeroo* and two more unnamed bombers. The 501st BS departed Nadzab Four and was led by Lieutenant Henry Kortemeyer flying *Outhouse Mouse III.* He dropped over the target at 4,000 feet, and was followed by *The Eager Beaver, Meany, The Gay Mare, Herky, The Wolf Pack, Minnesota Bomb Toter, Quitch* and one new unnamed bomber.

The 38th BG Mitchell crews had been briefed the previous evening that their target was supplies stored in Stuber's Plantation near Hollandia, which they would attack from 7,000 feet. They jumped off the back of trucks near their Mitchells early in the misty dawn at Nadzab Three. There they stood around bleary eyed, until just before 0900 when an officer in a jeep recalled them to the squadron headquarters hut. To a backdrop of other departing aircraft, these crews were given an updated and urgent briefing. Racing back

1 The load comprised ten "parafrags" which were 23-pound fragmentation bombs with parachutes, a Fifth Air Force hallmark since their introduction in late 1942. By 1944 they were ejected from a container which weighed 30 pounds, hence the total load of 260 pounds.

A 405th BS B-25H strafer with green dragon artwork at Nadzab around the time of Black Sunday. Six Mitchells from this unit participated in the 16 April 1944 mission.

A mixture of D and G model B-25s on their way to a New Guinea target in early 1944. A total of 42 Mitchells from the 38th and 345th Bombardment Groups were involved on Black Sunday.

to their Mitchells, they hurriedly departed just behind their *Air Apache* counterparts at 1015. The group launched six 71st BS B-25Ds, six 405th BS B-25Ds, six 822nd BS B-25D/Gs, two 823rd BS B-25Ds and four 823rd BS B-25Gs.

Six bombers per squadron does not seem many, however it is useful at this juncture to understand the demanding nature of the logistics which curtailed aircraft availability. In addition to repairing combat damage, the Mitchells required daily inspections, and more thorough 25-, 100- and 400-hour inspections. By way of example on 1 April 1944, the 405th BS had twenty Mitchells on charge, of which five were offline for inspections and engine changes. Due to its large-scale participation in the previous Hollandia raids of 3 and 12 April, by 13 April the squadron had nineteen on hand, however fourteen were unavailable for maintenance reasons. One was placed back in service the day before the raid enabling the squadron to launch six on Black Sunday.

The 38th BG Mitchells joined the three 345th BG squadrons over the Markham Valley, before meeting their Lightning escorts over Burui. They would hit the target at 1317, before returning via Burui at 9,000 feet which they planned to reach at 1403.

Like all Fifth Air Force units, the 38th BG had adopted squadron-themed markings, painting the noses of their bombers with the heads of dragons, wolves, panthers and tigers. Leering green dragon heads draped most 405th BS Mitchells led by Captain John Collins, with only two carrying nose-art: *Shitus Detailus* and *Grass Cutter*. The six Mitchells in the 71st BS formation included *Sweet Jeanne, Kings Cross Katie* and *Rosie the Riveter*. The 822nd BS led by Captain John Thompson included *Flying 8-Ball, L'il Ed* and *The Beast*. This latter had recently been transferred into the squadron from the 22nd BG which had named it, and on today's mission it carried cameras as well as bombs. However, this squadron lost two to aborts: Lieutenant Harold Popham turned back at Gusap with engine trouble, and then Lieutenant Henry Timmermans did the same over Burui. The 823rd BS included *The Lewd Lady, Polecat, Fer-De-Lance, Duchess* and *Old War Horse*.

The Lightnings

After their dawn breakfast, the *Satan's Angels* pilots at Nadzab boarded jeeps and bumped downwards over the John Britt Bailey bridge which straddled the pebbly Erap River. The journey took them past Fifth Air Force Headquarters on a nearby hill, down to Nadzab One and the group operations shack. A briefing officer said that the mission was probably cancelled, but to remain on standby. A quick change ensued: the mission would proceed but departure was delayed until weather cleared. With little to do but wait some pilots tried to relax in the shack's army cots, while others wandered out to repeatedly inspect their shiny new "J" model Lightnings. Here and there someone relieved himself of the coal-black coffee served at breakfast. Then the Lightning pilots stood by and watched the Liberators and Mitchells take to the air. Their relatively faster airspeeds meant the P-38s could afford to depart last. All three 475th FG squadrons would participate, the 431st, 432nd and 433rd FS. Only two 8th FG Lightning squadrons, the 36th and 80th FS would fly.

The Lightning pilots strode to equipment tents, collected parachutes stencilled with

The commander of the 80th FS, Captain Jay Robbins (centre), with his P-38J *Jandina III* which he flew on Black Sunday.

their names, checked jungle packs, then collected oxygen masks and helmets. Jeeps then dropped them off at the rear stepladders on the gondolas later retracted by crew chiefs after they had assisted their pilots into cockpits. After take-off, Dick Kimball, leading the 433rd FS banked shallow left, before glancing back to see the rest of his team roll down Nadzab Three. In Kimball's lead flight were Jack Purdy, Louis Longman and Lewis Yarbrough. The three flights behind included Lieutenants Carroll Anderson, Jack Daly, Austin Neely, Stan Northrup, Alan Pomplun, Joe Price, Clarence Rieman, LeRoy Ross, Pierre Schoener, Howard Stiles, Robert Tomberg, Mort Ryerson and Calvin Wire. The 433rd FS included Lieutenants Warren Cortner, Herb Cochran, Milton MacDonald and William O'Brien. The 432nd FS, led by squadron commander Captain John Loisel, included Lieutenants Henry Condon, Dale Burgess, Cliff Mann, William Elliot, James Farris, Jack Hannan, Robert Hubner, Jack Luddington, Elliot Summer and Captain Art Peregoy.

Tomberg was flying his one hundredth mission and he would recall that this coincidence had made him uneasy. He had confided such to his crew chief beforehand, who then offered to ground #177, but Tomberg persisted and was there at take-off. Black Sunday would deliver the 475th FG the hardest blow of any group in the Fifth.

The commanding officer of the 36th FS, Captain Don Campbell, departed at 1020 leading twelve Lightnings from #20, his assigned aircraft. The eye-catching moose on the aircraft's nose was unique, depicting Campbell's nickname. As he led the Lightnings over New Guinea's northern coastline, he noted that the weather over the Bismarck Sea and on the way to the target looked ominous. More Lightnings departed. The 80th FS dispatched nineteen colourful machines led by commander Jay Robbins in *Jandina III*, including *Betty, Classy Chassis, Copperhead, Corky IV, Helen, Hill's Angels, Lazy Lady,*

Longford Pat, Nulli Secundus, Peggy's Pegasus, Screwylooie, Staten Island or Bust, Sweet Sue, Uncle Cy's Angel, Widow Maker and *Yawn Patrol.*

These were followed by a mixed formation of Lightnings, comprising four each from the 431st and 432nd FS, which retracted gear at 1030. This formation of eight would escort the F-7As at high altitude. The last collective of Lightnings to depart was sixteen 432nd FS aircraft, launched at 1100 to escort the 312th BG A-20Gs.

After take-off, 433rd FS Lightning pilot Lieutenant Carroll Anderson noted:

> Visibility was unlimited, except for a few scattered cumulo-nimbus. I munched on a candy bar and tried to make myself comfortable in the cramped quarters of the cockpit. The life-raft oar in my chute casing did not help my sitting position any.

The A-20Gs

At 1035, the 3rd BG despatched three of their four squadrons from Nadzab; the 8th, 13th and 89th BS each with nine aircraft, leaving the 90th BS behind to perform overdue maintenance. Aircraft in the 8th BS formation included *Peggy, June, Weedoodit III, Miss Possum, Dunk's Junk, Kathleen, Queen of Heaven* and *Bub's Brother*. On the noses of the 13th BS aircraft, led by Major Richard Walker from *Powerful Katrinka,* was an emblem of the squadron "Grim Reaper" logo, a white skeleton advancing with a bloodied scythe. Walker's followers included *Joy Baby, Patches, Tiney Might, Lady Jacqueline, Mary Anna, The Taxpayer's Pride, Scotch & Soda* and *Honeybunch*. These A-20Gs were to bomb and strafe Hollandia's airfields from 1,000 feet and lower.

Powerful Katrinka's particular task, however, was to photograph the road connecting the airfield complex with the port facilities in the bay. *Powerful Katrinka* had been field-modified by Walker via the installation of a seat behind the pilot above the bomb bay so that a navigator could be carried. Performing the role on this particular mission was Lieutenant Donald Lees, the squadron's most experienced navigator. As the 13th BS circled to form up, Walker was aware of just how heavily loaded his squadron was with full fuel and bombs:

> Forming up such a large number of aircraft in the confines of the Markham Valley was a problem. The outer flights were pulling more power to stay in formation whilst the inside aircraft were making efforts not to stall out.

The 89th BS was led by Captain Walter Heyer, although he was not the squadron commanding officer at the time. As he climbed his squadron, Heyer was bracketed by *Milk Ear Willie* (Charles "CJ" Anderson) and *Jew Louie II* (Lieutenant Rade Vukelic). Behind them were *Joe the Joker, Hot Horse Herbie, Judge Goldfobber, Tobias the Terrible* and *Educated Edmund.*

From Saidor only two 417th BG *Sky Lancer* A-20G squadrons would participate: the 672nd BS and 675th BS, both cranking engines at 1045. These two squadrons had moved to Saidor from Dobodura less than a week ago, and hence were relatively unfamiliar with the area. Uniquely, they were operating with two gunners, whereas the other two

675th BS A-20Gs line up for take-off on a PSP runway at Saidor in April 1944. A dozen A-20s from this squadron flew on Black Sunday.

The artwork on *Hot Horse Herbie*, one of nine 89th BS A-20G Black Sunday participants.

A-20G Groups had decided this was a superfluous policy, increasing the chances of more casualties. The 672nd BS departed through scattered showers, and included *Fightin' Cock, The Big Assed Bird, A Touch of Texas, St Theresa, Tain't Funny, The Duke, Naughty Nancy, In The Mood* and *The Kitten.*

Captain Alfred Moser led a dozen 675th BS A-20Gs from an unnamed A-20G with the tail letter K. Accompanying him were Lieutenants John Simmons, Robert Mitchell, George Young (*The Green Hornet*), Paul Lucas, Harold Kohart (*Demon Express*), Michael Jovanovich, Duane Aamodt, Roy Andermann (*Sack Time*), Edward Davidson, Thomas Grimes and Robert Hedlin. Sergeant George Ertzbischoff, the lower gunner in *Sack Time,* later wrote that the weather was dull, and storms were in the offing. Saidor, unlike Gusap or Nadzab, lay on the coast, and in fact the weather there deteriorated in the absence of the departing aircraft. The rain became heavier from mid-morning onwards.

Finally, three *Roarin' 20s* squadrons, the 387th, 388th and 389th BS, departed Gusap at 1105. The fourth squadron, the 386th BS, was rostered off for maintainance. Included in the 387th BS formation were *Benny's Baby, Bevo, Pistol Packin' Mama, Shu Shu Baby, The Nervous Virgin* and *The Texan*. The 388th BS was represented by *California Sunshine, Sweet Li'l Kitten, Lady Constance, Little Doc, Mischievous Mary, My Akin Back, Old S* (flown by 312th BG commander Bob Strauss), *Rough Stuff* and *The Hell'n Pelican II*. The 389th BS A-20s included *Strictly Eager!, Je Reviens, Lak-a-Nuki, Little Joe* and *Queen Of Spades*. The wait had been particularly tedious for these three squadrons. Whilst their briefing had been conducted at 0700, departure did not eventuate for almost four hours. An intense blackjack card game killed time for many in the 387th BS, with one stake exceeding 1,000 dollars. As the delay lengthened, the players peered westwards down the Markham Valley, and comments were made that late-afternoon thunderheads would build like clockwork.

First Loss

With overcast still hiding the mountain peaks surrounding both sides of the Markham Valley, the waiting 22nd BG Liberator crews were expecting to return to their tents when word came to go. Lieutenant James Rayzor launched with the 408th BS from Nadzab at around 0900 and for the first half hour all went to plan. Then unexpectedly, just as the formation passed Gusap, Rayzor pulled away. He broadcast that his engines were giving trouble and he would land at Gusap. As soon as engineer Sergeant Milford Cummings was told about the problem, he jettisoned the bombs then closed the bomb bay doors as the bomber descended. Cummings warned the others to brace for a crash landing as they were too low to bale out, then returned to the cockpit where Rayzor told him he had shut down three engines due to faulty superchargers. This mystified Cummings as the superchargers were unimportant at low altitude, nonetheless it was too late to restart them, and the single remaining engine would not keep the Liberator airborne. The bomber descended too steeply for a controlled landing and crashed about a mile short of the north end of Gusap's runway.

Sergeant Asa Hatch, the left waist gunner, was one of the crash's three survivors. He was also a stand-in crew who hadn't flown with the others before. While waiting for take-off he kept pretty much to himself. Shortly after take-off he plugged in his headset to hear crew chatter. Hearing nothing of importance Hatch removed the headset and settled back for the long haul. The tail gunner suddenly appeared in the bomber's mid-section and Hatch could see that he sensed things weren't right. Then Cummings appeared and told them to brace themselves against the forward bulkhead. The impact ruptured the rear fuselage, throwing the lucky ones clear. The broken bomber came to rest near an Australian anti-aircraft battery, whose men were first on the scene. When Hatch came to, he found himself lying in the foetal position covered by a section of broken wing. He was covered with engine oil, his parachute had spilled, and his injuries included shattered teeth, cuts to the body and face, a broken left foot and puncture wounds to both knees. Tail gunner Sergeant Lawrence Dickson survived with a severely lacerated leg, together with the third survivor Cummings. The three were taken to Gusap base hospital for treatment.

The remains of Rayzor's 408th BS B-24J 42-109975 after it crashed about a mile short of Gusap.

Aborts and Premonitions

With more than 300 aircraft airborne there were bound to be mechanical problems. Leading the *Jolly Rogers*' 321st BS was B-24J *Kay-O*. Abeam Madang, faulty fuel line seals to the inner port engine caused 100-octane fuel to seep back into the fuselage through the waist gunner's hatch. Captain Bird shut down the offending engine, but the leak persisted. *Kay-O* returned safely to Nadzab after one and a half hours airborne. Then a *Red Raider* B-24J turned back just short of Lake Chambri, about halfway to target. Pilot Lieutenant Don Remillard had experienced difficulties including low hydraulic pressure, while taxiing at Nadzab, but had nevertheless elected to go. Once airborne, his difficulties worsened, and squadron leader Colonel Jim Sweeney ordered him to return. On the way home Remillard encountered the embryo front, which he described as a wall of clouds. He descended to tree-top height and returned to Nadzab along the coast via Finschhafen, taking only four minutes to pass under the forming front. When they approached Lae the crew discovered gunner Sergeant Hager Blair was trapped in the nose-turret which refused to swivel. The bombardier cut him out with a fire axe before touchdown.

As the formations headed for Hollandia eight 110th TRS P-39Q Airacobras and a similar 82nd TRS formation were returning to Gusap from an early morning barge hunt along the northern coast towards Tadji. At their debriefing the squadron's intelligence officer recorded indications of a solid front moving up. These Airacobras had been despatched to harass the enemy along the coastal roads west of Saidor towards Alexishafen, one of them was flown by Lieutenant John DeVore:

> As we saw towering cumulus move in, we scooted for home. By the time we were nearing the upper Markham Valley we could hear calls to Saidor tower indicating emergencies. When we heard two or three emergencies calling at the same time, we knew things were bad . . .

Lightning pilot Lieutenant (later Major) Calvin Wire of the 433rd FS who aborted the Black Sunday mission because of fuel transfer problems.

Well on their way to Hollandia, two 80th FS Lightnings also experienced mechanical problems, and were soon back at Nadzab. The first landed at 1225 with petrol siphoning from a main wing tank, the other with a troublesome starboard engine supercharger. Fifth Air Force policy was that all aborting aircraft were to be escorted home, unless close to base. Lieutenant Jack Hannan of the 432nd FS became fever-ridden *en route* and turned back for Nadzab where he was hospitalised. Meanwhile "CJ" Rieman of the 433rd FS, had a brand-new pilot on his wing. Twenty minutes short of Hollandia the newcomer lost hydraulic pressure, so Reiman fell in to escort him for the lengthy trip home.

Two other 433rd FS Lightnings also turned back: Lieutenant Calvin Wire and new pilot Mort Ryerson when Wire experienced fuel problems. Wire, who had turned 30 the day before, was flying a brand-new J-15 which housed two reserve 45-gallon tanks in the outer wings. It was desirable to use this fuel first to give the fighter better ability to manoeuvre. Both engines of Wire's Lockheed died approaching the rendezvous area and his hand scrambled for the fuel selector. Switching between tanks produced intermittent results so Wire radioed his boss Kimball that he had a problem. Kimball ordered him home with his wingman while he still had positive fuel flow. Wire then told Ryerson he had a "Snafu" on his hands, and confirmed he was still operating on the slung belly tanks, before the two banked for home.

The Mitchells and A-20Gs had been luckier, however. Whilst the Mitchells experienced no airborne aborts, mechanical problems grounded one *Air Apache* 500th BS Mitchell and two from the 822nd BS. Only one of the 88 airborne A-20Gs – one borrowed from the 90th BS - turned back due to an engine problem. The three A-20G groups, each having departed from different locations, were to rendezvous with the Mitchells at Burui near Lake Chambri, approximately half-way to the target, along with their Lightning escorts. All would not occur as planned, however.

While the *Sky Lancer* and 3rd BG A-20Gs met the Mitchells at Burui, the *Roarin' 20s* A-20Gs were late and lagged behind all the way to target by some 40 minutes. Thus, *Roarin' 20s* commander Colonel Bob Strauss navigated his three squadrons separately to Hollandia. On the plus side, his pilots were especially fuel conscious. Having flown to Hollandia twice before, with each mission having lasted around five and three-quarter hours, they were aware how closely they would be pushing their endurance. More wary than most was 389th BS pilot Lieutenant Gordon Gerould. During A-20 transition training in the US he had mismanaged fuel, which resulted in a crash landing. The incident had earned him the sobriquet "Crash Gordon", and he was firmly resolved that it would not happen again. *En route*, Gerould noticed that his main fuel gauge had not moved despite exclusive use of the main tank. He kept tapping the telling instrument as the formation droned onwards. Fortunately, the problem later proved to be a faulty gauge.

Navigation Overshoot

Leading the combined and forward formation of six A-20G and seven Mitchell squadrons was the 8th BS, commanded by Major Chuck Howe, flying A-20G *Here's Howe*. Among his pilots were Lieutenants James Brown, WL Wright, Milton Kellum and Herbert Rothery. Escorted overhead by *Satan's Angels* Lightnings, the A-20G formation flew lower than the Mitchells, at staggered altitudes from 1,500 to 3,000 feet. As they passed Dumpu, Howe flew approximately due west inland for an hour, then slowly turned right a few degrees at a time as they progressed. In the rear gunner's compartment of Howe's A-20G was intelligence officer Lieutenant Rignal Baldwin, aboard as observer. Following his map closely, Baldwin figured they were too far inland. He urged Howe repeatedly on the intercom to change course to a more northerly one, but Howe persisted.

As the looming hill ridges and coastline bordering Hollandia became more clearly defined, the crews saw that they had overshot the target considerably, having reached the shore east of Wakde Island (see the map on p.36). Howe led a wide 180 degree turn left to back-track inland, then climbed the formation to 6,500 feet, paralleling the mountain ridges to the south of Hollandia, before turning left again to 045 degrees and descending over the mountains to attack. The error had depleted 45 minutes of invaluable fuel. Leading the 8th BS second flight, Captain Andrew Weigel's diary reads:

> Major Howe became lost and went 100 miles beyond the target.

Also nervous in the same formation was *Sun Setter* co-pilot Lieutenant Lawnton Howell:

> We knew we were in trouble and went into low gas consumption mode right after getting back over land.

Leading his 13th BS, Major Richard Walker also knew something was amiss:

> ... the mission to the target was uneventful until we reached the crucial turning point. My navigator tapped me on the shoulder and pointed to his map and then to the terrain that identified the turning point. Howe did not alter course, however. We were operating under radio silence and so no-one made a comment. Finally, someone broke silence and informed Howe we were a considerable distance past our turning point. When Howe finally did alter course, we attacked the target from a different direction than had been planned. My squadron had to double back in order to get to the starting point for my photo run.

This navigation error, bad as it was, would be exacerbated by other issues which would

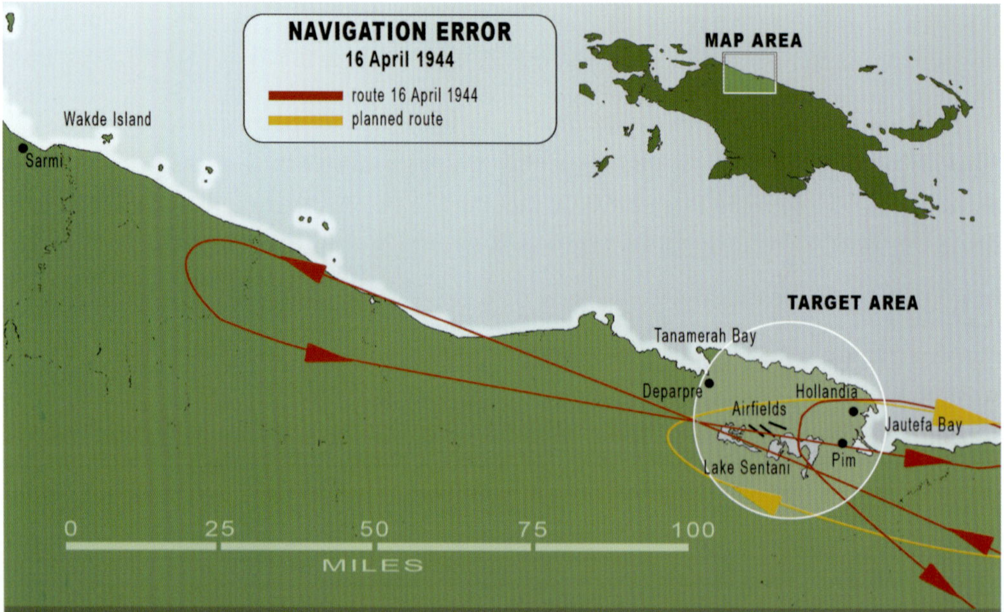

The planned route to approach the Hollandia target area versus the actual one on the day, taken by the combined forward formation of six A-20G and seven Mitchell squadrons. After a navigation error by the formation leader Major Chuck Howe of the 8th BS, the extra distance flown incurred a good hour's extra flying time, exacerbating later losses due to fuel starvation.

also consume fuel. The larger the formation, the more power and hence fuel required for lagging aircraft to catch up. The wide extra turns meant those on the outside of the turn had to fly at almost full power to catch up while those on the inside throttled back considerably to prevent overrunning the leader. Furthermore, some of these and later manoeuvres involved descent through cloud. In this configuration full RPM and higher speeds approaching 200 miles per hour were applied to assist tighter formations, thus incurring more fuel consumption.

In waves of six abreast, Howe descended the A-20Gs across Hollandia's runways whilst the B-25s did their job from medium altitude. Opposition gunfire remained slight and inaccurate, with luminous orange tracer reaching out from Cape Tjeweri, but falling short of the attackers. Captain Edmund Fowler led one of the three *Sky Lancer* A-20G flights over Hollandia:

> As we approached our target, it was noted that there was a complete lack of enemy aircraft stationed around the target strips. I thought at the time that they had possibly been decoyed away by one of our other units involved in the strike. There were no obvious targets with the exception of a lone tow-tractor being driven by a single Japanese soldier down a runway. We opened fire with our forward guns and released our bomb load hoping to damage the runway areas. A later review of our aerial photos showed the tow-tractor still going down the runway, but the driver had departed for parts unknown. We pulled away, got back into formation and headed for home.

Soon Strauss' *Roarin' 20s* caught up and made their attack. As predicted, enemy resistance was still light, and the Hollandia complex was soon obscured with smoke and debris. Much higher up the Liberators also dropped their payloads and turned for home. The *Jolly Roger* combat narrative records:

> A total of 66 tons was dropped in the supply and adjacent areas to the shores of Humboldt Bay. The pattern started in the water and trained inland through the assigned areas. Fires were started near the jetty with smoke rising to 2,000 feet.

Out to sea and much higher up, Major Joe Davis's F-7A converted Liberator photo-ships had arrived according to plan. Sensing that the main bombardment was over, remaining Japanese anti-aircraft crews resumed positions, waited and squinted upwards. To effect complete photographic coverage, Davis led his squadron for six minutes at 12,000 feet northwest to southeast, before turning 45 degrees and flying for another six minutes due east.

There was, however, an unexpected surprise. The resultant flak was the heaviest experienced by the squadron to date. First hit was Lieutenant Royce Harms, a burst jolting both inboard engines of his unnamed blue Liberator. The starboard one lost power immediately, but Harms and his co-pilot found that despite two cylinder heads having been shot off, it delivered reduced but adequate power. Meanwhile another burst ripped the fuselage and inner starboard engine of Lieutenant Loren Barstow's F-7A, but rendered no damage to the flight controls. Their job done, the big blue machines banked past the black puffs of flak and established a course for home. As predicted, no fighters had risen to meet the attackers. Not one Fifth Air Force aircraft had been lost in the attack. Apart from the damage to the F-7As, the flak and ground-fire had been less than during the previous Hollandia raids.

The Front - "Fascinating to See"

Broken into six scattered formations and with some scattered stragglers, the participants headed home. Liberators were first, followed by *Air Apache* Mitchells and their Lightning escort. Then came the *Roarin' 20s*, followed closely by Chuck Howe's large strung-out A-20G contingent. Separately and high above were the six F-7As, whilst each of the eight F-5 reconnaissance Lightings made their own way back. The shepherding Lightnings had no enemy fighters to contend with, and with a long return ahead had time on their hands. In their cockpits, and with the final Hollandia mission under their belt, many felt exuberant. 433rd FS pilot Carroll Anderson was escorting the *Air Apache* Mitchells:

> Dick Kimball led us into a rat-race in and around the bombers. With each pass the tail gunners and waist gunners could be seen smiling and waving to the fighter pilots as they sped by. Later, external belly tanks began to run dry and here and there a P-38J would lag momentarily as an engine stopped and windmilled until the pilot could direct new fuel into it. Then the engine would belch black smoke, sputter, take hold and pull the aircraft back into formation. The innocent rat-race caused excessive fuel consumption in the planes of the rear flights as each pilot had attempted to hold his position by the use of high manifold pressure and RPM. As the black smoke pall over Hollandia fell behind, it became obvious that thunderheads loomed ahead. As visibility worsened, anxiety replaced boredom. The front was white and silver and

A paint-stripped 8th PRS F-4 reconnaissance Lightning. The factory haze blue paint reduced the cruise speed of all reconnaissance Lightings by ten mph, and by April 1944 nearly all F-4 and F-5s had been stripped down to natural metal finish. After their completing their reconnaissance mission over Hollandia, the eight F-5s participating on Black Sunday flew independently back to base.

At Gusap, Lieutenant John Frost sits on the wing of the 39th FS P-47D he flew on the Black Sunday mission. Three 35th FG squadrons took off, but all were recalled to base due to the deteriorating weather.

> black and fascinating to see, but at the base where it wisped into the heavy foliage of the jungle, it was black and mean-looking. It stretched from the mountains to the south, and to the north as far as we could see.

The first indication of serious trouble came by way of rapid and nervous radio chatter between Liberators. The message was clear - the entrance to the Markham Valley, the only route home to Nadzab, was blocked. The closer the formations approached, the more urgent the radio calls.

Approaching the front from the other direction were three squadrons of 35th FG P-47D Thunderbolts, the 39th, 40th and 41st FS. The commander of the 39th FS, Major Harris Denton, had enough experience flying in New Guinea to be wary of such weather. The Gusap-based squadron's Thunderbolts were short-ranged compared to the Lightning. This meant they could fly only half the mission: Denton's sixteen Thunderbolts had launched late from Gusap at 1222 in order to rendezvous with incoming B-25s at Tadji to escort them home from the strike. However, the squadron was airborne barely an hour, returning to Gusap at 1330. Shortly after their departure the front ahead consolidated quickly, and soon the Thunderbolts were flying into the wisps of overcast. Forced lower and lower to stay clear, a choice had to be made whether to try to climb up through and over the turbulent weather, or to simply turn back. Denton chose the latter course, wheeling the entire squadron back down the valley and home to Gusap where he faced questions from several aggrieved young pilots who felt he had chickened out. The major cut short the inquisition with a statement that the decision was solely his responsibility which he fully accepted.

As it turned out, the sixteen 40th FS Thunderbolts which launched at 1253 returned to Gusap exactly an hour later when recalled by 19th Sector Fighter Control because of the weather. Also returning were the sixteen Thunderbolts of the 41st FS tasked to escort home the incoming A-20Gs. These Thunderbolts ventured the furthest from home base, reaching Annenberg before being recalled. A handful of these became separated from the main formation and made their way to Saidor or Finschhafen instead of their home base at Gusap.

From this point onwards events blur. To attempt to arrange the individual unfurling misfortunes of Black Sunday chronologically is unworkable. Within the next two hours aircraft would disappear, ditch, crash, be abandoned mid-air, force-land in hostile areas, or be destroyed or damaged in landing accidents. Many airmen would spend that evening fitfully in alien jungle, pondering the proximity of the nearest enemy. Others would drift all night in a dinghy without sleep, injured but alive. At Saidor hospital the wounded including those badly burned would be treated, but several would not survive. The last survivor would not return for another two weeks, with a final tally in human cost of 54 lives lost. The man at the top, Lieutenant General George Kenney wrote in his memoirs:

> That night there was gloom in the Fifth Air Force . . . It was the worst blow I took in the whole war.

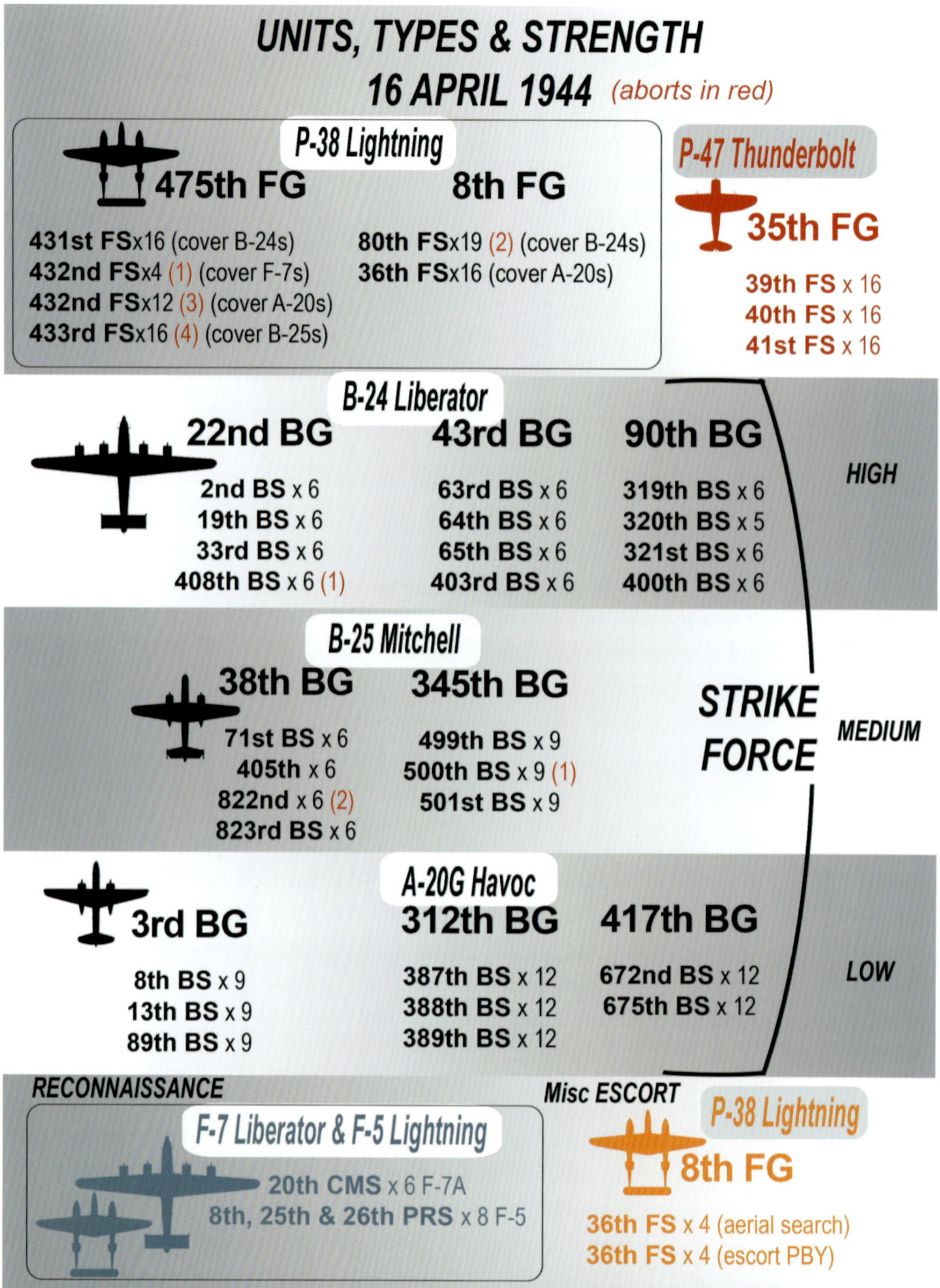

A full list of the combined Fifth Air Force Black Sunday participants. Over 300 fighters, bombers and reconnaissance aircraft were involved.

CHAPTER 3

LOST LIBERATORS

The first to encounter the towering front on their return were Liberators whose crews saw that the associated low-level cloud not only extended well inland, but that mid-afternoon convection currents had evolved the thunderheads into monsters. Those aircraft fortunate enough to have a navigator aboard logged a ten-degree rise in air temperature as they approached the front. Leading the *Red Raider's* 2nd BS was Colonel Jim Sweeney who, like all others in his squadron, had only limited experience on Liberators. The squadron had converted from Mitchells barely weeks before, and Sweeney was commanding only his third Liberator mission. He advanced all four supercharger levers slowly and raised the bomber's nose to climb. Behind and alongside in formation carefully followed the five others of the squadron. Things got worse. On Sweeney's wing, pilot Lieutenant Bill Amos observed that at 22,000 feet the frontal clouds were still a good 15,000 feet above them. A following 2nd BS Liberator was *The Lemon*, piloted by Lieutenant John Hellstrom who now decided they had no idea with respect to the magnitude of the frontal system. The Liberators were not oxygen-equipped and maintaining close formation in the jolting turbulence risked mid-air collision. Spotting a gap in the cloud, and glimpsing water at the bottom of it, Sweeney broke radio silence, and told them to follow as he dropped his squadron downwards in a tight spiral as recalled by Amos:

> ... we finally reached 150 feet and could see out of the side of the plane, but rain obscured the front, so I flew on instruments while co-pilot Major Chips Allen looked right, telling me when to ease away. We heard fighters calling maydays for ditchings ... we did a straight-in approach to Saidor and had to pull up a little to avoid masts from ships off the end of the runway.

Air and ground crew of the 2nd BS pose with Liberator *Redhot Ridinhood* at Nadzab at the end of April 1944. This late model B-24D was among those led on Black Sunday by squadron commander Colonel Jim Sweeney. Like all of the other 2nd BS pilots on the mission, Sweeney had limited experience flying Liberators as the squadron had converted from Mitchells just weeks earlier.

With no navigator aboard, Hellstrom meanwhile became separated in the dive and soon had no idea of his position. He was anxious about fuel, especially since the unforeseen climb. Now on his own, Hellstrom negotiated a dim shoreline, squinting through the rain for familiar landmarks. With gnawing uncertainty about their fuel, Hellstrom debated with co-pilot and engineer whether or not to ditch, but the consensus said no. Then Saidor airfield materialised through the gloom. The rain made visibility so poor that three approaches were required before they could line up. After landing and just before engine shutdown an engine quit from fuel exhaustion.

Meanwhile the six 33rd BS Liberators were led by Lieutenant LA Perraud from *Our Gal III*. One of his following Liberators was flown by "Scrappy" Evans, a light-framed man who had somehow emerged from the jungle after being shot down in late 1943. "Scrappy" had since acquired the unfortunate reputation of being a hard-luck pilot, and came close to losing his Liberator, navigated by Lieutenant John Mullady:

> We entered the front at about 10,000 feet and were on instruments. Shortly thereafter we encountered a fierce downdraft. Control of the aircraft was lost and "Scrappy" directed the crew to bale out. I attempted to do so, but the forces were so great that I couldn't move. I decided I was going to die in the next few seconds. We were suddenly flying straight and level at 200 feet above the ocean. "Scrappy" later recounted that at one point the ASI had read 400 miles per hour, but took no credit for saving us. Since that mission I became more nervous about the weather than the enemy. It was a disastrous day.

"Unsettled New Guinea Jungle"

After the loss of Rayzor's crew when it crashed at Gusap (see Chapter 2), the *Red Raider* 408th BS was down to five Liberators. These were led by Major Rufus Miller and flown by pilots Lieutenants Robert Stone, Dwain Harry, Thomas Paschal and Dunn. When they encountered the front, Miller steered them east, directly towards the Bismarck Sea, where he hoped he could descend safely with his squadron. The turbulence and cloud made sure keeping formation was difficult. Lieutenant Dwain Harry, flying *Lost Angel*, later submitted:

> ... we entered thick cloud at approximately 1445 hours. Lieutenant Robert Stone, in ship #42-110000 was seen to leave formation, making a steep turn to the right. At approximately 1505 hours I moved up into No. 2 position in "A" flight. Several minutes later we passed through an exceptionally dark cloud formation, and when we emerged Captain Paschal was no longer in formation.

Paschal had received orders that very morning promoting him to captain and was a pilot with considerable navigation experience. He had delivered one of the 22nd Bombardment Group's original Mitchells across the vast Pacific Ocean delivery route. Stone meanwhile had pulled away from the formation, mindful of a mid-air collision. However, water seeped into the aircraft's electrical system, short-circuiting the radios and rendering them useless. Then the vacuum system failed just after 1600, toppling his artificial horizon. Stone skilfully climbed his Liberator to 18,000 feet using the compass and airspeed indicator, a challenge for the most skilled pilot given the circumstances. Stone stabilised the bomber then ordered his crew to jump, and was last to leave. The crew, trained to pull ripcords shortly after exit, had a long ride down from 18,000 feet or so, eventually tumbling into the dense trees of the Finesterre Ranges. Bombardier Lieutenant Truman Henderson later submitted:

> There was snow and sleet at 18,000 feet that day. I landed on a mountain side of unsettled New Guinea jungle. I fired three shots from my .45 hoping to gain contact with the rest of the crew, but received no answer. That night I sent up a flare and got no answer, so thought the crew either dead or widely scattered. I spent the night sitting under undergrowth in a downpour of rain. The next morning I decided my closest contact with our forces lay in a northwest course to the sea. A large river ran through the jungles in this direction, and I decided to follow it. I spent the night under the roots of a large tree. I was wet, cold, and unable to sleep at all. I knew that by now my sisters had been notified I was missing in action, but was confident I could win through.

Two days later Henderson encountered friendly natives who on 23 April handed him over to US forces. Two days later a barge took him to Saidor, and he returned to Nadzab by C-47 next morning. Meanwhile it took seven days for searchers to find Stone, by then reduced to crawling on his hands and knees. Assistant radio operator James Egan arguably underwent the worst ordeal, however. He eventually stumbled onto a road inland from Saidor, after clawing his way through jungle for fourteen days. The rest of Stone's crew, with two exceptions, were returned to Saidor within a week or so after similar ordeals. However, co-pilot Lieutenant Harry Franklin and engineer Private Americo Picucci remain MIA.

The *Jolly Rogers* - "Lesser of Three Evils"

Similarly confronting the wall of cloud, the *Jolly Roger* Liberators likewise realised they were in for a skirmish. Lieutenant Nelson Stuart was a 400th BS bombardier:

> When we ran into weather everyone was on their own. A P-38 on command radio asked for landing instructions. He was told Dumpu, Gusap, Finschhafen were low ceiling and visibility. He responded that he would bale out on ETA.[1] Saw no other aircraft, then our flight indicator went out. We almost hit what looked like a PT boat. We were getting ready to ditch, the crew had the life-rafts out, but we got through to Lae with 30 minutes fuel remaining. I got out on solid ground, on hands and knees, and kissed it. A truck took us back to Nadzab.

Captain Morgan Terry led his five 320th BS Liberators in trail formation skirting wispy stratus, straight down the Markham Valley as low as he dared, directly under the towering front. He was flying a new and unnamed Liberator. Nonetheless the crew called themselves *Terry's Pirates* and affectionately referred to their bomber as *Weezie*, due to the unusual sound of its engines. Terry's crew had already flown four missions to Hollandia, so they were confident about this one until they hit the front. Tail gunner

1 Estimated Time of Arrival, meaning the pilot was preparing to bale out just before he expected to run out of fuel.

The distinctive *Jolly Roger* insignia of a 90th BG Liberator at Nadzab, seen just a few days before Black Sunday.

Dick Grills sometimes peered back into the fuselage as they came down the valley, to see how the side gunners were faring. He recalls that when the gunners saw how low they were, they stood there scared to death as they occasionally passed a geographic outcrop. That evening Grills played poker late into the next morning to unwind. Sergeant Allen Welton was the nose gunner of *Sad Sack* which followed Terry, whose Liberator logged seven hours seventeen minutes for the mission:

> We came down the Markham just off the top of the trees. You could smell the steaming swamps and jungle. We were about 200 feet off the trees, but it seemed as though we could pick the foliage from them. And the rain beat down about us. I was about to drown before I could slip out of the turret. One slight turn in that storm would have probably dashed us into a hill of the mountain of either side. Once we started there was no turning back. To turn meant to kiss a hill and leave an unmarked grave, if the rain and erosion were kind enough to give us one. You can't go through one of those storms, nor are you supposed to go under. You are supposed to turn back. But the enemy lay around us and home was dead ahead, so we took the lesser of three evils. And we came up scared but smiling. It broke just a little way above Gusap, so we lined up five abreast and buzzed the airdrome at Gusap and I guess those boys will long remember the day B-24s tore out of the storm just passing over five abreast. The boys' eyes at Group about popped out of their heads when we broke out of the storm into the clear right over their airdrome.

Here 'Tis Disappears

Meanwhile four 403rd BS Liberators were also trying to get through. They were led by Captain Erwin Zastrow from *Sack Bound* when Major Russell Bragg became separated and decided he would try for Port Moresby. Glancing intermittently at his instruments, Zastrow at first poked about the face of the front at high altitude before deciding that they were using too much fuel. Unable to find an opening, he shelved any idea of getting home to Nadzab and ordered the other three to proceed individually to Saidor. It was 1500, and Zastrow estimated their position as approximately 35 miles west of Madang.

On his starboard wing was B-24D *Here 'Tis*, flown by Lieutenant Raymond Cooley, an inexperienced young pilot flying his first combat mission. Zastrow instructed Cooley to take a heading to Saidor and proceed by himself. Cooley acknowledged and was last seen climbing east.

Lieutenant Raymond Cooley flew B-24D *Here 'Tis* on Black Sunday which went MIA but was located post-war in the Finesterres. Pictured is Cooley's crew during training in the US. Top row left to right: Cooley, co-pilot Lieutenant Dudley Ives, navigator Lieutenant George Archer, bombardier Lieutenant Donald Grady. Bottom row left to right: engineer Technical Sergeant Richard Sargent, Staff Sergeant Norman Nell, Technical Sergeant Steve Zayac, Staff Sergeant Thomas Knight, Staff Sergeant Joseph King and Staff Sergeant Blair Smith. All ten of these men were lost aboard *Here 'Tis* on Black Sunday.

Saga of *Sack Bound*

Zastrow's decision to split up his flight was made under duress. Among his crew were co-pilot Lieutenant Hayden Clark, left waist gunner Sergeant Bob Roth, and radioman Technical Sergeant Bill Solomon. *Sack Bound* had dropped eight 1,000-pound bombs on Hollandia which, when they exploded, jolted the Liberators from as high as 10,000 feet. Their crews could only wonder what it felt like for the enemy. Having descended low, Zastrow steered *Sack Bound* into the gloom towards the coast. His reasoning was that he could conserve fuel by using the "ground effect" of flying low over water. From his left waist gun, Roth noted that clinging to their wing was another white-tipped 403rd BS Liberator, a Mitchell, and an F-5A. As this unhappy team droned onwards Roth noted that:

It was raining so hard that the pilots could see nothing. From the waist windows we

> could see ahead a few hundred yards at times and at other times we could not see the wing tips. Whenever the soup looked too green, we would tell Zastrow to pull up. Sometime later we noted the F-5A was gone. Later we noted the Mitchell was no longer with us. After going into an area of zero visibility we came out alone.

Towards the front was radioman Bill Solomon:

> … at times I could see our right wingtip almost touch the white caps on the stormy waves as we were buffeted by the force of the wind. The radio was jammed with Mayday calls, mostly from P-38 pilots running out of fuel. We had enough to get to Finschhafen, but not enough to fly over the mountains.

Sack Bound overflew the unfolding chaos at Saidor then came into relatively clean air just short of Finschhafen where the bomber landed after eight and three-quarter hours airborne. After conducting the traditional ground-kissing ritual, Zastrow's crew realised how hungry they were. Finschhafen had almost no facilities, but they fortunately had parked within a few feet of an anti-aircraft battery whose crew shared their supper. That night was spent bedded down on their flying gear underneath the Liberator's high wings. Dexter Fairbanks, another *Ken's Men* Liberator pilot, would remember the mission as the one he flew exactly three weeks after his 24th birthday:

> The storm between us and our base was a monster, too thick to go through, too wide and too high to go over. The wing formation broke up then group formations broke into squadrons and eventually we received word to proceed home individually. Another pilot in my squadron and I decided to stay together. We turned west for a while, found a hole and let down over the jungle below. From here we headed north flying right on the deck. Upon reaching the coast, I would guess at a point somewhat west of Madang, we headed east along the beach. We were flying at a very low altitude, probably under one hundred feet, which was necessary in order to maintain visual contact with the shoreline. Shortly the storm became so intense that I broke from the other B-24, as it was impossible to fly with another aircraft and keep sight of the shoreline. My intention at this time was to head for Saidor, however the traffic on the radio soon made it apparent that this would not be wise. All you could hear were requests for a fix or a course, pilots getting ready to ditch, or who were just plain lost and pleading for help. Aircraft were smashed up all over the strip at Saidor. I had a quick conference with my engineer concerning our fuel, and with my navigator concerning our location. Neither conversation was very productive. As we continued down the coast the storm seemed to lessen somewhat. My navigator and I figured we could make Finschhafen or Cape Gloucester, but with Gloucester being closest, we headed for it. Eventually we hit land, followed the shoreline north and landed at Cape Gloucester at 1415 hours, rendering a total flight time of eight hours and thirty-five minutes. This was approximately an hour longer than a normal mission to Hollandia. The following morning, we took on fuel and flew uneventfully back to Nadzab. All in all, it was quite an experience, something that will be with me forever.

Major James Pettus was flying *Shirley Anne* in the 65th BS second flight. With twenty missions under his belt, Pettus quickly judged that the front was well above any altitude that he could climb. The squadron circled near the front looking for an opening before the leader radioed they should all head for Saidor at low altitude. Experience had shown Pettus that the cloud base of New Guinea's thunderstorms was about 600 feet. He decided that under the circumstances Saidor would be too crowded. Besides, the extra distance would severely test his bomber's depleted endurance. Pettus had confidence in his judgment and decided to try for home alone. The turbulence would be bad at low altitude in the valley, but nothing compared to trying to drive directly through the front above the mountains. He also judged that the other pilots, who lacked his flying experience of New Guinea, could not safely conduct what he was about to try. Not wanting them to follow he feigned engine failure by feathering an inboard engine, radioed he would head for Nadzab alone, then banked and descended under the front:

> We restarted the engine and took a good look at the map. The river ran direct to Nadzab and there were no mountains over the river. Next was to drop the gear, slow up, crack flaps, run up props to 2000 rpm, go into auto rich and instruct the navigator what to do - he was to keep the river in sight at all times and give directions to me and the co-pilot as to how I was to steer. Co-pilot was to keep the altitude level at hopefully 500 feet, but we could go lower. The navigator indicated with hand directions whether to go left or right a few degrees. We dropped down to 500-600 feet where the vertical visibility should have been good and headed into the rain which was in solid sheets. The vertical visibility held but we still went a little lower. Airspeed was about 130 mph, with wheels down and flaps cracked. It was a nerve-wracking 40 minutes or so until it began to lighten up and soon the rain eased off. A few minutes later we saw Dumpu, and I had a real qualm that the AA might shoot at us as we came close to the strip. By this time the sun was out, and we made it home in good order. We were the second B-24 to get to Nadzab. Two other 65th BS planes came down the valley but had a very rough trip in and out of cloud. They arrived well after we did.

Seated behind Pettus and his co-pilot was Technical Sergeant Samuel Commons, *Shirley Anne*'s engineer, who strained his eyes looking for breaks in the cloud. He wrote that evening that the surrounding mountains were not ones to be trifled with, especially in a storm. By the time *Shirley Anne* reached Nadzab's circuit area the No.2 generator had gone and No.3's prop governor had failed. The mission marked Commons' thirteenth, and henceforth he regarded the number as a lucky one.

Lieutenant Robert Hanks was the co-pilot of another 65th BS Liberator which elected to continue with the others, but soon lost them:

> We were on instruments when we suddenly found ourselves in a very large cavity in the clouds. Here we completed several turns and during the course of turning two P-38s attached themselves onto our wings whilst others were doing the same to other B-24s. We did not have radio contact with the fighters, so finally we wagged our wings and flew in a straight line across the cavity and back into cloud with the fighters attached to our wingtips. Our navigator directed us out over the water where we descended. When we arrived opposite Saidor the fighters broke away whilst we continued to base.

In a similar dilemma in the nearby 65th BS formation was navigator Lieutenant Joseph Esposito, who had to shout instructions to pilot Captain Marcus Carroll, such was the din in the rain-battered cockpit. When he judged they were clear over the ocean he advised Carroll to make a 180-degree let-down at approximately 500 feet per minute. The Liberator broke out eventually over the water at 300 feet and then Esposito directed another 180-degree turn until they found the coast. Carroll then followed the coastline to Finschhafen, proceeded past Lae, and then westwards along the Markham Valley to Nadzab.

F-7As – Nadzab at Last

The six 20th CMS F-7As (call-sign "Scarlet"), were last to leave Hollandia led by squadron commander Joe Davis from *Little Joe.* Accompanying him were the others flown by pilots Lieutenants Royce Harms, William Wilson, Loren Barstow, George Rives and Ralph Brower. After accomplishing their mission, they approached the darkening front at 8,000 feet. To their advantage, each F-7 had extra fuel reserves provided by two extra 600-gallon tanks installed in the front bomb bay. The first to return to Nadzab was named *T.S.* whose co-pilot Lieutenant Ben Woodall recalled:

> I could see many aircraft of all types flying around at low altitude, in all directions like a swarm of disorientated birds. It was rather a sobering sight. I figured at that point there would be losses.

Davis saw a valley which looked like an escape route and climbed his squadron into it. Then the crew of *T.S.* lost sight of the others, although they remained in tight formation. There was turbulence, slashing rain, and no way of telling where they were. Davis ordered the others to try on their own, nonetheless two F-7As nevertheless stuck with him. *T.S.* banked swiftly left down to a mere hundred feet altitude above the coastline. Northwest of Saidor a lone P-47D pulled in close, most likely one of the several 41st FS ones which became separated after their abort near Annenberg. The co-pilot Woodall switched their SCR-522 radio set to the fighter frequency in time to hear the Thunderbolt asking whether they could jettison a spare life-raft so he could ditch. Woodall replied they could, but that Saidor was not far. The anxious Thunderbolt pilot thanked them and veered away. *T.S.* continued along the coast, past Saidor to Lae, then turned right over the mouth of the Markham River and found Nadzab. They had been airborne eight and a quarter hours.

Another F-7A was *Rip Snorter* whose navigator was Lieutenant Jay Robbins (no relation to the 80th FS commander Captain Jay Robbins). He recorded that night that the ocean was whipped into white caps by the wind, and that both Brower and his co-pilot fought the controls. Staff Sergeant Challen Wells was one of *Rip Snorter*'s gunners:

> Sometime after leaving Hollandia, I was busy in the photo compartment either working on my photo records or writing a letter to the woman I was to marry upon my return home. We encountered a rough flight. I didn't pay much attention until Sergeant Hein came into my compartment and said that Brower had announced over the intercom that we were to prepare to abandon ship. I reached for my chest parachute to discover that it would not fit my harness. I always wore the harness -

The artwork on F-7A *Rip Snorter*, whose navigator was Lieutenant Jay Robbins. After a rough flight back from Hollandia the Liberator made an unplanned landing at Saidor. One of the K-17 camera ports is visible on the bottom right.

> both harness and 'chute had snaps instead of ring and snap. Uncle Sam had made a design change, and I had grabbed the wrong type of 'chute before the mission. I walked aft and looked out the waist window - a 'chute wouldn't do any good here - we were in a tropical storm - at 200 feet altitude with high waves - too low to jump and it would be like going from cauldron to fire. It was time for a spell anyway, so I moved to the tail gun position. Harms' F-7, which had been hit over target, was following us. We proceeded cautiously down the coast. An aircraft suddenly appeared out of the cloud behind us. I charged my guns - it was a P-47 and shortly afterwards we picked up a P-38. They stayed with us all the way to Saidor - misery loves company.

In a wet gloomy tent at Nadzab, *Red Raider* pilot Lieutenant John Broomall waited impatiently for the return of his comrades. He had not been rostered on the mission, but Broomall knew from the panicked radio chatter that his friends were in trouble. Broomall had earned an instrument rating before the war and convinced his superiors that he could assist. Against good advice he departed in a B-24J and flew through the front and into the clearing behind Madang where he found circling Liberators. They latched onto his wing, and he brought them home.

Lawrence Wulf was a 19th BS Liberator pilot who was also off duty. His diary records the fate of all six of the squadron's Liberators: three returned to Nadzab about 1800, about an hour later than expected. One landed at Port Moresby, one at Saidor and the other made Finschhafen. It was extraordinary that a Liberator decided to head as far away as Port Moresby, the furthest available airfield in New Guinea that day. Yet Major Russell Bragg, the 403rd BS commander also put his Liberator down there. Jack Shelton was flying another 22nd BG Liberator which made Saidor:

> When we all got back to the entrance of the Markham Valley, there stood one of the most massive fronts that any of us had ever seen. It was very distinct in its formation and towered skyward some 70-80,000 feet, being a cotton white at the top, shading down to an inky black at the surface. Immediately behind the front was an area of clear visibility in which aircraft were milling about, all running low on fuel. All were travelling at varying speeds and the whole thing kinda resembled a big airport with no control tower. This left every man for himself. Planes were ducking and dodging each other, with a near miss every second or two, all the while trying to make up their mind as to what to do. The final decision was simple - either penetrate the front or run out of gas and attempt a forced-landing in the marshes below. We in the B-24s were the lucky ones, as we had more gas on board than the others. But we didn't have all that much, and the moment of decision was at hand. I decided to suck in my gut and prepare to fly through it. With the decision made, I dropped down to just above the water's edge to re-set my altimeter and climbed back up to about one hundred feet. I was aware that the only way to freedom was just to bust into the front; hang on and hope for the best.
>
> I lowered my landing gear, then cracked the flaps attempting to try to go as slowly as possible in the turbulence. My seat belt was already tight, but I re-tightened it; said a big prayer and entered the inky black wall. We hit a broadside of water, but it wasn't as violent as I had expected. The water built up on the windshield to the point that the wipers just sat there and vibrated, unable to move. After about ten or twelve minutes in this cauldron (which seemed like an eternity), it began to lighten up and we finally emerged from the storm and out into the daylight, still in one piece. After all that, I thought we had the worst of it behind us, but we still had a more dangerous situation confronting us. That situation was the landing at Saidor, a super-short metal runway that was hard to approach. Also, it was never built to take on as many airplanes as it did that eventful afternoon. We finally got down safely, although blowing a tire in the process and coming within a hair from running out of gas. All in all, it was quite an experience, with no repeats, please, and it still remains a chilling memory to this day

Technical Sergeant Glenn Wright was the radio operator aboard Shelton's Liberator:

> My thought going to the target had been - why are we bombing there again? - I was on the 12 April mission and there had been nothing but rubble that I could see. It looked the same today ... when we hit the storm, it was a wall of water. I didn't see another plane until we saw the strip at Saidor. The pilot said he dropped down to one hundred feet, but it looked more like fifty to me. After we got close down to the water, we could see the New Guinea coastline. I don't know how long it was until we saw the airstrip along the coast. It looked awfully short to me, but it was a place to

land. We had to make two passes to land. The first time we had one wheel over the airstrip and the other over the mud. I was sure thankful when we pulled up and went around and made a good landing except we blew a tire. They managed to keep us on the runway and when we got stopped we were at a place where the mud wasn't too bad, and we got off the runway. We had to have a tire flown up to us and put on before we could leave to go back to Nadzab. After getting back to Nadzab and getting to my tent, Hager Blair, with his morbid sense of humour, had hidden my clothes and my cot was gone. He said he thought I had gone down in the ocean. He knew better and I never forgave him.

A typical Fifth Air Force camp area at Nadzab – which must have seemed heavenly for most of the Black Sunday crews struggling to find a way home. This belonged to the 345th BG in mid-1944.

Colonel Clinton True sits in 500th BS B-25D *Tinkie*, named after his wife's nickname, which remains MIA. The bomber, flown by Lieutenant James Waggle, has never been located and likely crashed into the sea.

CHAPTER 4

SCATTERED MITCHELLS

After their medium-level bomb drop, the three *Air Apache* squadrons led by Captain Dale Speicher remained around 8,000 feet and settled in for the long journey home. Just above, and sometimes playing through their formation were *Satan's Angels* Lightnings. As they flew closer, Speicher judged that returning home to Nadzab through the towering mass was feasible. Shortly after entering the front, the escorting Lightnings were nowhere to be seen. In the murk, their departure was barely noticed by Speicher's focused and apprehensive crews, now either flying on instruments or following flight leaders. Very soon the deteriorating visibility had separated many. Ahead lay the only gap in the front, a narrow fissure of relatively clean air positioned directly over Cape Croisilles. With hastily reassembled formations, Speicher climbed them to 10,000 feet towards it, hoping to locate a break. Nervous crewmembers caught the occasional glimpse of Astrolabe Bay and its sandy coastline below which Speicher descended towards. The loose *Air Apache* formation spiralled downwards. In the rapid descent, aircraft again became separated and reformed with others at the bottom, not always from their own units.

Tinkie Vanishes

When they pulled out above the treetops, the formation had become a strung-out series of loose and unidentifiable flights. The 500th BS which had launched seven Mitchells that morning, pulled out at high speed above the tree line in loose assembly. However, when they levelled out Lieutenant James Waggle's *Tinkie* was not there and remains missing to this day. Now down on the deck, the remaining six 500th BS Mitchells placed themselves in two V-shaped formations. When Captain Hobart Rankin's six touched down through the dark drizzle at Lae, they had been airborne for seven and a quarter hours:

> I led the men about two miles offshore until viz deteriorated to about one and a half miles, and the ceiling was dropping with constant rain. Some pilots started getting concerned about fuel, so we leaned out a little and slowed to 180 mph, putting the ships into a wider formation - two ships to my right and three to my left. I flew a time and distance problem to be sure I could get them between Karkar and Long Island, and the New Guinea coast. We tightened formation and came closer to land. As we approached Saidor I told them we would take a look, and each could make their own decision on going in. We were abeam of the field and about three quarters a mile offshore when we witnessed a head-on collision and ball of fire on the runway. We continued in tight formation, eventually adjusting heading to round Finschhafen. All altimeters were reset to 50 feet, my estimate of the height above the sea. We turned towards the Markham River mouth. By now it was dark, and we had our running lights on. The rain was getting heavier, so I let down, telling my guys to stack up on

> me. At 20 feet I saw the sea and levelling off, proceeded towards Lae, completely dark but rain easing. I spotted the lights of Lae. We all made it but were happy to pat the ground. I am sure the only reason I can relate this is because God had a hold of my flying suit.

Meanwhile seven 501st BS Mitchells led by Lieutenant Henry Kortemeyer had also levelled out after descending through the break over Cape Croisilles. Kortemeyer gently turned them through driving rain along the coastline in two closely knit flights, the second led by Lieutenant Tom Lewis. Lieutenant William Davis was among this formation when both engines started surging. He left the formation and descended, ordering his crew to prepare for a ditching. Then he saw a B-24 in the distance with gear down and decided to follow it instead. An uneventful landing at Finschhafen completed Davis' afternoon.

Included in the Kortemeyer formation was *The Eager Beaver*. Its port engine suddenly ran dry and its crew prepared for ditching just when they broke out of cloud near Saidor. The bomber put down safely on one good engine at Saidor, slashing the starboard main tyre. At this stage the squadron further fragmented, when *Meany* and an unnamed Mitchell with a Donald Duck logo broke left, headed for New Britain and landed at Cape Gloucester. Late on the afternoon of Black Sunday, Kortemeyer's 501st BS was a rare and fortunate exception: by that evening all of its aircraft were accounted for at Finschhafen, Saidor and Cape Gloucester. After the squadron refuelled at these different locations the next morning they regrouped at Nadzab the following day where they discovered that the film in all three of the squadron's K-21 cameras had been ruined by soaking rain.

Stingeroo Ditches

After the hurried squadron approached Cape Croisilles, Captain Richard Baker's nine 499th BS strafers reformed and hugged the coast in three flights abreast. All made Finschhafen, except for *Stingeroo*, a modified B-25D strafer being flown by a replacement crew. After leaving the target, its starboard engine had developed an oil leak. Standard practice was to feather the propeller while oil pressure remained, then shut down the engine before it seized, however Lieutenant James MacWilliam decided to take a gamble. Well behind enemy territory, it seemed safer to try and keep it going to keep up with the others, especially since *Stingeroo* had no navigator.

However, his luck ran out during the rapid descent down the cloud canyon when the propeller slipped into fine pitch, badly yawing the aircraft left. To avoid a mid-air collision MacWilliam pulled out of formation to sort out his problems. Friction from red hot crankshaft thrust bearings ignited hydraulic fluid, however, which set the engine on fire. The heat's potential to melt the mainspar left MacWilliam no choice but to ditch; he feathered the good engine, jettisoned the top pilot hatch, and fully lowered the flaps. The Mitchell settled firmly into the swell and filled rapidly with sea water, steam hissing off its engines.

The struggle to clear the sinking bomber saw a mad scramble by the five crew who quickly exited and inflated the emergency dinghy. Looking around, the new seafarers could see they had ditched between Karkar and Bagabag Islands, north of Madang. Assuming correctly that both cloud-shrouded mountainous islands constituted Japanese territory, they decided to keep their distance. Aboard the dinghy was an emergency radio which they cranked. They had no fresh water, but it was drizzling. Survival packs yielded chocolate bars and malt tablets in the dark, and they spent the night drifting in a choppy swell, draped with a parachute to keep warm.

Baker's eight Mitchells meanwhile had continued eastwards following the littoral of a darkening coastline. Aboard one of these bombers was radio operator Technical Sergeant Donald Hitchcock:

> ... it had been a bouncy flight all the way but got progressively worse. Normally I did not keep my seatbelt buckled except on take-off or landing, but this was getting a bit much. I could see out the small windows near me that the sky was getting dark - almost a blue-black colour - which even in a temperate climate indicates a severe weather condition. The turbulence tossed us around like a kite, and the belt strained against my lap. I was pushed down heavily at some point. I was told later my pilot had pulled up sharply when an island appeared out of the gloom dead ahead. At one time he called me on the intercom to see if I could get a weather report from anyone. The static was so severe that I couldn't even hear my own signal to tune it. The pilot accepted my explanation without any question. He was probably having the same problem on his voice radio that I was having on my Morse system. After what seemed like an eternity the shaking, pitching, rolling and tossing seemed to ease up. The sky lightened, and we headed for Finschhafen.

Sun Setters - Last to Attack

The *Air Apaches* had been the first Mitchells to negotiate the front. Behind them were four 38th BG *Sun Setter* squadrons led by group commander Colonel Larry Tanberg. These had been the last Mitchells over Hollandia at 1308. After the attack, all four squadrons became strung out at medium altitude, and initially headed for home in this loose formation. Their cruising speed was faster than the A-20Gs which they gradually overtook. Tanberg;

> This is one time we got caught. We went up and the front moved across and just socked in everything and it was a fiasco from then on.

In the 823rd BS Lieutenant Edward Poletrack was flying a B-25G Mitchell he had named *Polecat*, his nickname within the squadron. He descended the bomber to sea level along the coastline, taking turns to share the controls with his co-pilot. The blast through the windshield armour plate on the G model proved very loud and distracted both pilots. They found Saidor with about half an hour's fuel left, before executing a perfect landing on the wet metal strip. The navigator Lieutenant Alfred Colwell was flying his 48th mission aboard Poletrack's B-25G:

> On the way to the target, I was nervous as a cat and expected all hell to break loose, but we reached Hollandia, dropped the bombs and had no trouble. Still shaky, I decided I'd been flying too much so started reading a magazine. About halfway back co-pilot

> Ziggy "Jack" Jackowski tapped me on the shoulder and pointed ahead – south, east and west all socked in solid with black clouds, rain and wind. We had two hours gas left and it was one and a half home. The whole formation kept flying hoping for a hole somewhere ahead but soon we began to circle. The only clear spot was north but that was all Jap territory, as was the area over which we were circling. Around, around, up, down – the situation was getting no better fast. We'd been circling for an hour and now our only hope of getting down safely was to make Saidor, about 30 minutes away. The weather that way looked even rougher, but we would be over water most of the time. We had just decided to leave the formation and go it alone since the others all seemed to have more gas when suddenly we all spied a little hole just over the coast and the water. Everyone nosed down and dove for it. Just as we got over the water we hit rain and wind – couldn't see a damn thing. The whole area was full of planes. We got down to 50 feet above the coast and followed it toward Saidor.
>
> I directed "Polecat" (Pilot Ed Poletrack) right and left along the coast. He and Jack were both flying, dodging planes. Once our airspeed went down to 120 – it looked like we'd have to ditch any minute. Now and then we'd lose sight of the coast and weave back and forth along our course to pick up again. After 30 minutes of this we suddenly saw a strip just ahead of us. Jack dropped wheels and flaps and Polecat nosed her down for a landing – didn't have any idea how long the strip was or what was at the other end – couldn't see that far – but there wasn't much choice. Polecat never made a better landing, and we didn't slide at all when he applied the brakes. We taxied over to one side. It was raining to beat hell, but we piled out right in the middle of it ... I was drenched to the skin and beginning to feel sick. Caught a truck and went for hot coffee and something to eat. We couldn't find a place to sleep so seven of us finally went over to the hospital, put on a sick act and they put us to bed with a few sleeping pills for the night.

Colwell flew with scratch crews for the next several days kicking out food, clothing, blankets and medical supplies wherever they found suspected wreckage or downed crews in the jungle. They also conducted administrative flights between Nadzab, Saidor, Finschhafen and Gusap, and served on a funeral detail for one of the casualties.

In the 405th BS, Lieutenant Harry Terrell flew as a co-pilot whose bomber was airborne six and a half hours of which he logged two and a half of control time. When they finally put down at Cape Gloucester, they were joined by two 823rd BS B-25Gs. It was Terrell's 29th mission:

> Here's another day and another mission. Briefed after chow and took off at 1000. The weather locally didn't look too hot. We hit out on course and made our objective. Did an excellent job of bombing. Right on target from 6,800 feet. On the return leg we hit bad weather over the Finesterre Range this side of the Markham Valley so Eddie Maurer broke us off. Our flight buzzed over Madang and out to sea ... a P-38 would come up and fly with us for a while and then he would disappear. Every once in a while, we could see another aircraft going out somewhere. We paralleled the coast about 20 feet off the water to stay underneath the weather. Visibility was about

> one mile. The land was socked in solid, so we broke over land once and banked out steeply to avoid the hills. We almost lost sight of our leader. We broke out in the open and saw Cape Gloucester and headed in. As young pilots who don't realise a lot of things, we made a real big peel off which was the wrong thing to do because that bank angle uncovered the pump in the port engine apparently and we lost the engine and hit the feathering switch and continued on around and we landed after having our right engine cut out on the go around. We made a go around because of aircraft on the runway. We knew we were almost out of fuel. It was on the go around when we banked to get around again that we lost the engine. We landed on our second pass. Five B-25s and one B-24 set down there. We stayed with the 1st Marine Division – damn nice guys.

Pilot Lieutenant Edward Maurer was leading the 405th BS:

> The clouds were completely out of sight and just as black as it could be. It was a monsoon condition. It was like a roadblock across all avenues of escape, from the valley floor all the way around the horn to Finschhafen and around the corner to Lae and then over Nadzab and up over the Owen Stanleys. I started collecting planes, particularly the fighter planes. I remember the P-38s that had been covering us asking if they could stay in close to us to get them through the weather. The supply division of the Air Corps issued Polaroid glasses with at least five or seven different colours of Polarised filters. I found the most effective was almost an orange/amber colour. These would separate the weather for you – you could see in three dimensions. I wore them for occasions such as that, for instrument flying and for leading the group or the entire strike force because I could pick out the avenues open around the cloud tops. You wouldn't believe how much that sharpened everything up. It made a tremendous difference.
>
> I stayed down on the water, and it just kept getting blacker and blacker, but you could always see the whitecaps. We were flying so low the prop tips were actually picking up a vortex. There were some A-20s that were flying with us down with me on the deck and they swung out over the water to the right and headed toward the south following their lead plane. They didn't say anything. They didn't give any reason. They started picking up speed, and I wasn't in a race to get through this stuff. We were doing everything to save fuel. All we had to do was come around the corner and up past Lae and right up the Markham Valley and just stay down on the treetops. There wasn't anything in the way to hit then because it is all valley. That's what we did. The area was saturated with everybody trying to land at once.

Maurer's 405th BS formation included *Tokyo Sleeper* flown by Lieutenant William Bill flying his first command mission. Seated to his right was co-pilot Lieutenant Harry Terrell flying his 29th mission. Once they broke out into the open and saw Cape Gloucester, they headed straight for it. There they touched down on the second approach after the starboard engine cut out on go-around on the first.

Lieutenant Hugh Breneman became separated from his 71st BS buddies and found an LST

Green Dragon Mitchells of the 405th BS along the northern New Guinea coast. On Black Sunday several 405th BS B-25s found a way through the weather by flying low over the sea and eventually landed at Cape Gloucester on New Britain.

The PSP-covered runway at Cape Gloucester in April 1944, with 80th FS Lightnings taxiing for take-off. Several B-25s and a B-24 landed there on Black Sunday.

offshore which he circled and prepared to ditch alongside when his fuel was exhausted. Then a P-38 came out of a cloud directly in his path which he turned tightly to avoid but placed him in a position whereby he could see that Saidor was close by where he subsequently landed. Meanwhile the weather separated the six 71st BS Mitchells into two flights. Lieutenant Paul Popma led the first flight from *Seven Day Leave*, while *Sweet Jeanne* flown by Lieutenant Marshall Phillpit led the following flight. Phillpit later recalled:

> ... the weather was socked in zero-zero. I did not attempt to enter the cloud. I led my flight on the deck from the right wing. The radio was full of desperate calls. In as

> much as most of our missions were strafing ones, none of our instruments worked well. We had to use needle and ball almost exclusively. I had very little instrument time. It was tough for aircraft to keep sight of one another.

Lieutenant Lawnton Howell was the co-pilot in yet another separated *Sun Setter* Mitchell:

> Nearing the Sepik, we could see that the Markham Valley had cloud down to the valley floor. At first it looked like we could climb over - let down over the water to Lae, then back under overcast to Nadzab. As we were climbing, an A-20G came up behind and called for us to take him home - he was almost out of gas - we told him to stay with us, but he finally broke off at about 8,000 feet, saying he had to head for ocean in case he had to ditch. The cloud kept getting higher, so at about 10,000 feet we decided to swing northeast to get over ocean. When we were sure we were over water we started a slow descent heading east southeast, and finally broke out at about 100-to-200-foot ceiling. We set course for Saidor on low gas mode. We were at about 1,000 feet and commenced a straight-in landing for Saidor. A huge black cloud with rain in buckets completely covered the field. We decided to head for the emergency strip at Cape Gloucester. There were boats scattered in the Vitiaz Strait, and we figured if we had to ditch, one of them would pick us up. About two miles from Gloucester one gas tank was knocking on empty, and the other was close. We decided we had to do a straight-in approach or ditch. A B-24 landed ahead of us, stopped at the end of the runway and was slowly turning to taxi back to where the only exit taxiway was. I called the tower as we lowered our wheels and said, "We're coming straight-in" - the tower told us to go round - I said, "You get that son-of-a-bitch off the strip or we'll land on top of him - no gas to go round". The B-24 heard us and revved his engines. As we touched down our left wing barely missed his tail. We duplicated his feat getting back up the runway to clear a B-25 coming behind us. As we parked, we thanked the Lord we were spared to fly another day. We slept on cots underneath the plane and flew back to Nadzab next morning.

Captain John Thompson led the 822nd BS from B-25G *Lil' Ed*:

> I elected to go under while others tried to go over. We had no oxygen. At least six other Mitchells followed me, as did several P-38s. Aircraft were landing at Saidor in various states of wheels-up and wheels-down. There was mass-panic in the landing pattern, so I proceeded to Finschhafen, landed, refuelled, and returned to Nadzab.

Nose art and mission markings on B-25 *Seven Day leave*, from which Lieutenant Paul Popma led the first flight of 71st BS Mitchells on Black Sunday. The pilot is unidentified.

CHAPTER 5

A-20GS ON BORROWED TIME: THE *ROARIN' 20S* FRAGMENT

In the cockpits of their returning A-20Gs, *Roarin' 20s* pilots drank coffee from thermos retained by stainless steel straps to their left shoulder, and ate sandwiches. Formation was tight and they observed radio silence which was strictly enforced by their commanding officer Colonel Bob Strauss. A West Point "Ringknocker" graduate, Strauss took unkindly to offenders. The looming frontal mass indicated to Strauss that fuel conservation would be crucial. He descended the three participant squadrons of his group into the deteriorating visibility where they emerged in the bottom of a cloud canyon behind Madang. Many others of varying types had arrived here before them, and low on fuel, these stragglers were conducting wide circles to seek a gap. Strauss later commented:

> When we reached the hills separating us from the Ramu Valley the mist and light fog were down on the hill tops. I thought of heading for the coast and Saidor but I had no idea what the weather was like there. At that time Saidor was little more than an emergency strip and could not begin to accommodate the entire group. I commenced a wide circle at about 500 feet and throttled back. The rest were following more or less in trail, without trying to maintain formation because of the reduced speed.

Pilots found it strenuous to keep sight of each other in the poor visibility and trailing units began to fall behind. Major Bill Kemble, leading the 388th BS, knew that his outside wingmen were tracking wider turn circles, requiring more fuel to keep up. Kemble broke radio silence urging everyone to conserve fuel as best they could. Lieutenant Lee Anderson, flying 389th BS aircraft *Lak-a-Nuki,* was positioned on Strauss' outer wing, and felt creeping doubt they would get back. Anderson also sensed the outer flights were using more fuel than he was.

The rearmost 388th BS A-20s became the most fragmented. In trouble first was Lieutenant Joe Gibbons flying *Lady Constance* who had lagged badly behind the others since departing

Colonel Bob Strauss sits on A-20G *Old S* from which he led the *Roarin' 20s* 312th BG on Black Sunday.

the target due to an erratic engine, chewing up valuable fuel. Turning away from the formation Gibbons headed back towards a clearing he had spotted several miles back, then circled twice to inspect it. The first approach was aborted in poor visibility. On his second attempt the port engine, seized when it ran dry. *Lady Constance* hit a ridge and skidded left. The impact was violent, tearing the starboard engine clean from its mounts and buckling the fuselage. Gibbons' head was gashed, and gunner Orville Rhodes' arm bruised. The two set up camp nearby after taking all their belongings from the wreck and settled in for a dishearteningly long night.

Next to leave the strung-out 388th BS formation was outer wingman Lieutenant Charles Davidson, flying *The Hell'N Pelican II*. With both fuel warning lights on, Davidson offered gunner "Red" McKenna via the interphone the option of baling out or riding down on the aircraft. McKenna's answer was decisive to "stay" and he urged Davidson on with a "Let's go". Lowering flaps to reduce speed, Davidson approached a vast kunai grass clearing. The port engine ran dry as the A-20G mushed through the long grass after impacting tail first. It came to rest at 1715 close to a tree line leaving behind a flattened 300-yard swathe of crushed kunai grass. In the fading drizzly light both crewmen contemplated their fate. The distant drone of circling lost aircraft left an eerie impression.

Among this distant formation was Lieutenant Walter Bartlett flying *My Akin' Back* who had lost sight of the others. Already dangerously low, Bartlett eased the control column forward to go yet lower, hoping he could remain above the lush foothills below. A narrow river materialised and Bartlett, gnawed by dread, sensed he was somewhere behind enemy-held Wewak. He instructed his gunner to find a clearing so they could set down. A tract appeared ahead which looked like an airstrip, so Bartlett lowered the gear, skidded *My Akin Back* onto its surface, then cut both throttles. Soldiers ran towards the aircraft. A startled Bartlett threw open the hatch, then clambered back along the wet fuselage to the gunner's compartment where a loaded M1 carbine was stored. It was not needed. They had landed at Faita, an emergency landing field, and the soldiers were Australians manning an outpost.

Similarly, Bert Heyman had also pulled *Rough Stuff* out of the 388th BS formation. He found a river which was the Ramu, and fifteen minutes later was on the ground at Gusap after following the river's twisting littoral at tree-top height.

Major Selmon Wells, leading the 389th BS, was transfixed by the looming front which:

> ... appeared like a solid wall of weather - even the P-38s were making noises that they couldn't make it over the top. I decided to take my flight and try and get underneath it. We couldn't manage that either.

Wells headed for the coast instead, taking Lieutenant Charles Russell as one of his two wingmen. Wells found a lone Liberator scouring the coast, and reasoned it was better equipped to find a safe landing place than he was. Wells' flight tucked in very close to follow the Liberator, where they were joined by another 389th BS A-20G flown by Lieutenant Alexander Milliken. The four soon arrived over Saidor but it was too crowded for their liking, so they continued to Finschhafen where they landed just before dark.

A-20G *The Hell'n Pelican II* several days after it was put down by Lieutenant Charles Davidson.

Late afternoon at muddy Gusap on Black Sunday. Tail code K in the foreground is 388th BS A-20G *Rough Stuff* which Bertram Heyman has just landed and behind it an unidentified 13th BS A-20G.

Down Bales Out

A native of Texas, Captain Frank Smart led the 387th BS from *The Texan* identifiable by its colourful Texas flag painted under the pilot's window. Smart's squadron flew in wide circles with the rest of the *Roarin' 20s,* among which was Lieutenant Ed Bistika flying *The Nervous Virgin*. Bistika decided to brave it alone by following the wide Ramu River just above the treeline, eventually breaking into clear air near Dumpu. He eased into Gusap, logging six hours and 25 minutes in the air.

Back among the circling 387th BS A-20Gs, Sergeant Stewart Down was riding as turret gunner with Lieutenant Nicholas Daviscourt. After circling near the lower wisps of the front for what seemed a long while, Daviscourt also broke away to try to find a solo path. Soon their fuel situation was serious, however, and unsure of where they were, Daviscourt ordered Down to prepare to bale out. Then he suggested Down jump saying he would follow shortly afterwards. Down rolled out head-first through the bottom hatch and started counting to three. As he fell all he could see was "jungle and a small river". His senses told him he was very low, so instead he counted only to one and yanked the ripcord. Trees snagged his chute which broke his fall, but he found himself hanging in a tree just above swampy water. Following a series of misadventures friendly locals took him across the Ramu in their canoe, guiding him to Faita where he was given clean clothes and food. Australian soldiers there told him that late on Black Sunday, Daviscourt had overnighted before returning to Gusap early next morning.

Benny's Baby into Swamp

During the slow circling at the edge of the front, Strauss broke radio silence and ordered Smart to take his flight and find an opening. At this stage Smart was accompanied by Lieutenants Glen Benskin (flying *Benny's Baby*), Donald McGibbon, Robert Findley, Robert Smith and James Knarr. Unbeknownst to the others Benskin was overcome with difficulties; his radio was inoperable, a situation he tried to unsuccessfully communicate to Smart with hand gestures. Thick overcast permitted only intermittent glimpses of the rolling landscape below, and Benskin became convinced that Smart was lost. In fact, Smart had completely backtracked from the front and eventually encountered the coastline west of Uligan Harbour. Unable to hear any of the radio chatter, Benskin grew more frustrated, and boldly broke away to fend for himself. Among Smart's remaining five A-20Gs was McGibbon:

> Captain Smart was looking for the Ramu River, but we picked up the Sepik. By this time our gas was very low, and we decided to go to the ocean and make our way down the coast. At that time, I had nearly one hundred gallons of gas total. To get through the rainstorms we were forced to fly at minimum altitude over the water.

Well inland, Benskin became more disorientated, and he suspected correctly he was too low on fuel to reach anywhere friendly. He told his gunner, Sergeant "JJ" Westerman, that they would have to put down while ample fuel remained for a controlled landing. From a couple of hundred feet, the green area looked deceptively smooth, and it was only when Benskin flared did the full height of the kunai grass become apparent. *Benny's Baby* rotated a quarter turn clockwise before coming to rest at 1750, verging on sunset. The forward fuselage had been twisted by the impact, jamming the canopy shut. Westerman levered it open, enabling Benskin to squeeze through. Benskin later recalled:

> ... the first night was sheer agony - it was hard to believe that there could be so many mosquitoes in the world. At any given moment we were able to wipe hands down our sleeves and kill a hundred or so in one pass. This was in addition to the leeches which constantly attached themselves to our ears and lips.

The Texan Ditches

Meanwhile Smart's gaggle pressed on but soon lost each other in worsening squalls. Then

Lieutenant Glen Benskin who force-landed A-20G *Benny's Baby* in a remote swamp on Black Sunday.

An unidentified PT boat offshore Saidor in 1944. Some aircraft ditched in the vicinity of such craft on Black Sunday hoping for a quick rescue.

anti-aircraft guns fired at them when they passed by Uligan Harbour. Continuing onwards at low altitude and now almost out of fuel, at 1730 Smart requested ditching assistance on the emergency frequency. McGibbon watched Smart jettison his canopy, followed by the dinghy stowed just behind the pilot which was blown out by the slipstream. *The Texan* ditched smoothly. McGibbon raised Saidor and nearby PT boats clearly visible in the distance. Then he circled Smart and his gunner, Sergeant Mike Music, both visible in

Mae Wests. Findley joined McGibbon while one of the gunners dropped another dinghy. Findley exchanged radio calls with approaching PT boats, which acknowledged they were making haste towards the survivors. Smith, flying *Shu Shu Baby*, also witnessed the flawless ditching:

> I circled with the other two until I saw both crew safely in the life raft. Music waved to me, and we set off for Saidor. About ten miles away was a PT boat. I flew past, monitoring the distress signal and pointing my aircraft's nose in Smart's direction. I couldn't tune into the correct radio channel to communicate with them, and by this time my reserve tanks were reading empty, so I headed directly for Saidor.

There the men confirmed Smart's position with Air Rescue. Since the pair had ditched not far from shore, and neither appeared hurt, there was expectation they would soon be ashore. Smith made subsequent inquiries with operations, but no-one had knowledge of Smart's whereabouts.

Collecting Stragglers

Unlike their *Roarin' 20s* counterparts which initially tried to stay together as a group, the 3rd BG left the target later and were split into two separate formations by the wall of weather. Whilst the 13th BS broke off for the coast and Saidor, the 8th BS and the 89th BS pressed ahead through the Ramu Valley. Captain Andrew Weigel led an 8th BS flight of six:

> The weather appeared threatening near the Tadji area along the coast. I turned inland at Vanimo and began picking up additional aircraft southeast of Wewak. There was a 200-foot ceiling and heavy rain. By the time we approached the Ramu Gap into Dumpu we had accumulated about fifteen A-20s, but there may have been more behind which I could not see. We never entered cloud. On approaching the gap towards Dumpu I saw a large number of 312th BG aircraft ahead, not in formation, seemingly flying around looking for a way out. I made no radio calls. When I saw them milling around, I knew what had happened. To the north of the narrow gap down the Ramu towards Dumpu is a wider and more inviting valley - which leads to the mountains. I had made the same error about a month ago. They had followed this route and were boxed in. These aircraft had attacked before us. How long they had been circling before us I do not know.

Australian infantry spotter Alex Perrin witnessed to this low-level flight:

> Fellow spotter Stan Carter and I heard the roar of engines, went out to investigate and saw this large number of Bostons [the Australian name for the A-20G] flying at about 50 feet along the Ramu Valley, heading for Gusap USAAF base. We were amazed at the noise - there were just under twenty planes that would have been in trail formation. The whole village population came out of doors to see what was going on, and we got straight onto the transmitter on "X" frequency to report the American planes, as it was so apparent that they were lost. Both of us got the jeep started up as we thought the planes looked as if they could have crash-landed at any moment. A couple of our boys lost a jeep and trailer later that day when the river came up so suddenly that they were washed off a crossing.

Weigel brought home six 8th BS A-20Gs plus three more from the 89th BS back to Nadzab where he landed with only 30 gallons of fuel. Led by Walter Heyer, the 89th BS pilots chatted on the radio to argue the best way home. In the event only three of this squadron made Nadzab. *Milk Ear Willie* put down at Dumpu, whilst the others put down at Gusap before their fuel gave out. Heyer recalled:

> Although the general consensus was to fly down the coast rather than to take the shorter route though the Markham, I decided on the latter. By flying as low as possible we were able to fly under the weather at a fuel-saving speed. Eventually we arrived at the emergency strip at Gusap. We landed there because of the possibility that we might not reach Nadzab with the limited fuel we had remaining. We spent the night at Gusap and continued to Nadzab the following morning.

Lieutenant Ralph Wandrey was based at Gusap with the 9th FS, then operating P-47Ds, when word came down that help was needed to try and guide stragglers back down the valley. Both Wandrey and 9th FS commander Major Gerry Johnson launched to spend the next three hours in their P-47Ds searching among the banks of clouds along the squall line where visibility was about two miles. The ceiling was about 5,000 feet at Gusap, but as they proceeded up the valley it gradually lowered to treetop level. They were about 25 minutes out when we saw a number of planes circling in one of the pockets of limited visibility. The pair made radio contact and Johnson told them to follow Wandrey home while he tried to locate others. Wandrey took this first group back to Gusap including several A-20Gs.

Major Chuck Howe, who had led the main low-level contingent over the target, led an 8th BS gaggle back to Nadzab. He proceeded to the phone in the operations tent and called his group commander to explain his navigational error. Rumours later circulated that he commenced the subdued conversation with "This is Private Howe speaking". Included with Howe's group at Nadzab was Lieutenant Dwight Turner who had flown *Weedoodit III*:

> It was the longest flight I ever made in an A-20. As I parked the airplane on its hardstand and shut down the engines our squadron Ordnance Officer, John Ransier, came alongside below the cockpit and shouted up to me that I was eligible for the Royal Order of the Purple Shaft (for having sat on a parachute cushion seat for that length of time). Our people on the ground had been looking for us to get back for quite some time.

Behind Japanese Lines

Major Richard Walker led the 13th BS which was among the last units to leave the target. Walker decided to stay over open water since he knew he could safely fly low with visual contact. His navigator Lieutenant Donald Lees replotted a course for Saidor and the squadron managed to stay together, with three exceptions. Two of these were Lieutenant Donald Dower and one of his wingmen. Dower radioed Walker requesting that the formation slow down to save fuel, however Walker was reluctant to do so as the turbulent weather challenged the nine aircraft to safely maintain formation. This consideration, Walker judged, posed a greater threat to safety than fuel shortage. Nonetheless Dower and the wingman slowed, a decision which would cost both as we shall see.

The third breakaway was Lieutenant Billy Sanders from Piggot, Arkansas, whose day had begun badly. A last-minute mechanical hitch saw his borrowed A-20G for the mission, *Joy Baby*, depart last. Sanders ran his engines at high power to catch up, with commensurate extra fuel consumption. Then in low cloud on the return Sanders lost the others. He picked his way low along the shoreline, unsure of his position. He knew that Saidor was ahead, but his fuel simply ran out. With both engines feathered and gear and flaps lowered, Sanders put down onto a narrow sandy section of shoreline. *Joy Baby* came to rest about a hundred yards inland, on the northern side of the mouth of the Malas River. The landing collapsed the nose gear, and impacted the starboard wing against trees, tearing off several feet.

Both crewmen were fortunately unharmed, and they were confident they had put down within Allied lines. In fact, they were stranded approximately 30 miles northwest of Madang, well inside enemy lines, and close to a coastal dirt road which ran just behind their aircraft, frequented by Japanese traffic between Madang and Hansa Bay. The two men built a shelter for the night, lit a bonfire to attract attention, and used fishhooks from their emergency kit to catch several fish before turning in.

Meanwhile back at Nadzab, newly arrived and off-duty 8th BS A-20G pilot Lieutenant Ben Rogala could do nothing but wait. Around him everyone viewed the tragedy as a preventable one, and a mission which should not have been authorised. Also rostered off was 13th BS pilot Lieutenant Joseph Brown who listened instead to a radio set in the operations shack, and the many frantic calls it received. When darkness descended not one 13th BS A-20G was to be seen. Brown wrote around midnight:

> I've often read about the dramatic hair-raising time when planes are missing and the ground crews were sweating them out, but this time it's really happened. The boys have been gone 12 hours now and not a word have we heard from them - they ran into bad weather - soup - and tried to make their way back to Saidor. God grant that our boys are safe. Some A-20s landed at Saidor, but no knowledge of which squadron they belong to. P-38s are going in all the way down the coast. Rumour has it that 35 airplanes are missing from the operation. Just heard over the radio that the search for survivors is called off until morning.

When the bulk of the incoming *Roarin' 20s* A-20Gs finally made Gusap's circuit area, those with the least fuel were allowed to land first. The 389th BS had some close shaves. Ed Hambleton's crew chief checked the tanks of *Je Reviens* after it shut down and told him that the only fuel he had left was in the carburettors. *Little Joe* lost the main formation but found Gusap where it rolled to a stop at the runway's end after both engines quit. The pilot Leonard Happ and his gunner got out and mumbled a thanksgiving. It had been a particularly bad day for Happ who had also run into machine gun fire from 3rd BG A-20Gs over the target.

Surprisingly *Lak-a-Nuki*'s crew chief measured 60 gallons in her tanks, and the ever fuel-conscious "Crash Gordon" Gerould still had 80. Nonetheless when darkness fell the whereabouts of thirteen of the group's aircraft was unclear. At the flight line, Lieutenant

Ewing McKinney conducted the 389th BS nose-count, establishing that four were missing, including the commanding officer Major Selmon Wells.

Six 387th BS aircraft were missing including squadron commanding officer Captain Frank Smart. The 388th BS was missing three, their location as yet unknown, including Walter Bartlett safe down at Faita (along with two other stray 3rd BS A-20Gs, including *Milk Ear Willie*). Nadzab's searchlights were turned on as beacons for aircraft which might still be airborne. That night radio propagation was poor and High Frequency radio communication was difficult. Radio calls from Saidor confirmed many A-20Gs had landed there, however their identity remained unclear.

Lieutenant Ed Hambleton's *Je Reviens* at Gusap. His crew chief checked the tanks after landing and told him he barely had sufficient fuel to fill the carburettors.

388th BS A-20Gs hold a tight formation on return from a Wewak mission. While some squadron commanders successfully led their formations through the weather on Black Sunday, many aircraft separated and found themselves alone.

CHAPTER 6

VANISHING LIGHTNINGS

On Black Sunday two Nadzab-based fighter groups placed 75 Lightnings alongside and overhead bombers they were assigned to protect, following nine aborts. Aside from the main force of escorting Lightnings, there were also two separate special missions, both conducted by 36th FS P-38Hs. The first was led by Lieutenant Orville Erdmann who, anticipating being on the last big Hollandia mission, had been disappointed when he discovered that his flight was assigned to escort duties. In this case it was a VP-34 Blackcat, a responsibility which would keep them well away from the target.

The second protection flight with callsign "Agate Special" departed after Erdmann's, led by Lieutenant Eugene Zielinski. Its task was to escort a single 822nd BS B-25G Mitchell flown by Lieutenant Charles Fisk which was to search the Sepik plain behind Wewak for the crew of a downed B-25G Mitchell from the same squadron. It had put down into a swamp inland from Wewak four days previously due to mechanical failure. Accompanying Zielinski were Lieutenants Walter Mikucky (pronounced *"Mikusky"*), Robert Keown (pronounced *"Cowan")* and Lawrence Reeves (flying a borrowed 80th FS P-38). The flight departed Nadzab at 1020 and reached the search area about an hour and a half later. The Mitchell's crew found the downed bomber, then searched the wide swampy area for nearly two hours. However, with no sight of the downed crew and seeing dwindling fuel reserves, Zielinski told Fisk he was heading home:

> We soon encountered a heavy overcast about 15 miles south of Annenberg that had gotten down to 1,000 feet and rain squalls. At this point I changed our course and headed for Madang, with the intention of landing at Saidor. When we reached the coast at Yalu Point the overcast was again down to 1,000 feet and a solid sheet of rain falling. With my flight still together, we headed out to sea in an attempt to find an opening in the clouds. Off Yalu Point we found a hole and circled for 20 minutes, and then I radioed my flight that I was turning to the left. My wingman Lieutenant Mikucky followed by element leader and his wingman, turned to the right. This was at 1440, and the last I saw of the element. With my right engine already feathered, I radioed my wingman, telling him that I was baling out and instructed him to do the same - it being impossible to get through the weather with a shortage of fuel. I baled out off Yalu Point from approximately 800 feet, landing in the water one and a half miles from shore. This occurred at 1500 hours. In a few minutes I was rescued by a barge, and was told that my wingman, Lieutenant Mikucky, had crashed into the sea and exploded about a mile away.

On board the barge was Jack Wallace, a 58th FG armourer based at Saidor:

> Two P-38s circled our craft and one of the planes crashed in the water. We got to the

> crash site, but all we found were an oxygen tank and landing gear. The other P-38 circled some more, then climbed, and the pilot baled out. We managed to pick him up. He was very badly shaken up. We then went on down the coast. We saw several oil slicks on the water where planes went down but found no survivors.

Meanwhile, trying to find the "Dumbo" PBY they were meant to be escorting, was Orville Erdmann:

> We flew at around 10,000 feet near Hansa Bay, and when looking back towards the Markham Valley it appeared black. We continued onwards trying to contact the Dumbo with negative results. All the time we were looking back and didn't like what we saw. Finally - after unable to contact Dumbo - we announced that we were returning home due to the weather closing in. Crossing inland from Hansa Bay towards the Markham Valley we knew we were for it. None of us had flown actual instrument weather - plus we were unsure how accurate our instruments were. I picked up the Ramu River and as the weather got lower and lower, we flew right down on the deck. When the weather approached zero-zero I put my flight in trail and flew right down the river, below the trees - when the river turned, I turned. After some time the weather lifted a little bit. I recognised the areas where the Ramu and Markham Rivers are fairly close together. I then picked up the Markham and flew along that, passed Gusap, and continued on to Nadzab. The ceiling there was about 700 to 1,000 feet. We heard chatter on the radio and knew some guys were in rough shape. We were some of the first back, landing around 2 to 3pm.

The commanding officer of the 36th FS, Captain Donald Campbell, led a contingent of sixteen Lightnings to escort returning A-20Gs, with Lieutenant Ralph Turri leading the rear flight:

> The cloud was in excess of 30,000 feet altitude, and it was a safe assumption that it exceeded 40 or 50 thousand feet. Its front edge was not clearly defined. We flew along the face seeking a thin spot to make reasonable penetration. We had limited instrumentation and limited experience. I considered splitting the formation and ordering my fighters onto the wing of a returning bomber, but they were evidencing as much concern as we were - due to their uncertainty they were milling about at various altitudes and going in all directions. There was much radio conversation. The transmission reflected the very real concern about the weather and possible actions. I gathered up my flight - I had eight when I departed that area. I noticed that the river to Lae was visible inland, so we went down and took a look. There was a ceiling and some forward visibility, and fuel had now become a factor. We went into string formation, dropped combat flaps for improved control at low speed, and followed the river. It was touch and go, but it worked, and we broke out before reaching Nadzab. I went to Operations, turned in a complete report, which included an Intelligence debrief. I do not recall the loss predictions but do remember that all my chicks were accounted for . . . we were lucky.

Satan's Angels

Among the 433rd FS Lightnings, weaving behind the Mitchells, were pilots Lieutenants Robert Tomberg and Carroll Anderson. Referring to their diaries, Anderson later compiled their joint experience:

> Into this beginning of chaos steadily moved Possum Squadron [the 433rd FS] and the Mitchell bombers . . . "Keep it in close - we'll try to go through together" - With that command from Kimball, I reached forward over the control yoke and uncoupled the artificial horizon and gyro compass, then checked the fuel gauges and leaned back the mixture control of each engine as much as possible. The P-38 was still using fuel from its external belly tanks, but they were very low and I knew it. I looked at the weather front again. It loomed above and around us, appearing even more alarming . . . within minutes every pilot of the 433rd knew he would have to fly on instruments to reach home. Carefully, Dick Kimball led the fighters into an apparent opening in the weather. Just as carefully, he turned and gently eased the squadron back out. The squadron was tucked in so tightly it was difficult to avoid collisions. The precision formation flying which Possum squadron had constantly practised was paying off. Another gradual turn into the weather and the first serious trouble developed. Flight leader Tomberg's flight became separated from the rest of the squadron by a thick layer of stratus. Unable to see the rest of the aircraft, and wishing to avoid the possibility of mid-air collision, he made his choice and led his flight away from the possible course of the squadron.

In fact, Tomberg's Blue Flight attempted to penetrate the front at 25,000 feet, then again on the deck, but turned around both times. They entered the front the third time at approximately 12,000 feet when Tomberg's electrical system went out. He tried to uncage his artificial horizon but pulled the knob off instead. Anderson's account continues:

> Hello Tomberg . . . this is Anderson . . . you are in a spiral to the left. Pick up your left wing. No answer. As the airspeed moved up close to 300 mph, the balance of the flight stayed in formation. Suddenly the flight swept out into the open in a deep canyon which was completely enshrouded with cloud. Schoener grinned wryly, waved his hand in a goodbye gesture and peeled off to try it alone. Tomberg looked back at my wingman, Joe Price, shrugged his shoulders and started back into the weather again. He really had little choice. The jungle below was impassable. In addition, it very probably was enemy-occupied. His choice was either to try and fly by the seat of his pants or die in the jungle below. Price and I followed Tomberg with grim confidence in his ability as a seasoned pilot, but completely unaware of the true circumstances of his so-called instrument flying. A few minutes later in a tight climbing turn, a P-38 stalled out and he spiralled away. As he did, I began calling Tomberg. "Hello Tommy. This is Andy. You are stalling me out. You are turning to the left and stalling me". No answer. Just before a complete stall, Tomberg's aircraft levelled, nosed downward into another spiral to the left. Once again, the P-38s were proving it was "Lockheed for Leadership". The airspeed built up to 375 mph and was still going up when the jungle flashed into view. I looked down for a second and saw cockatoos and flowers

> scattered among the treetops. It was close. Almost instantly after pulling out, we were back in the stuff. My plane suddenly stalled under 55 inches of mercury and maximum prop RPM, gradually falling off in a spiral to the right. Carefully, I brought the plane under control and began the delicate operation of flying a fighter on instruments. At the very moment I stalled away, Tomberg released his canopy and baled out. Japanese or no Japanese, jungle or no jungle, he decided it would be better to get out and walk rather than risk the presence of another cool, green mountain.

Tomberg reached on the wrong side to pull the ripcord, corrected the mistake and waited for his parachute to open. He then landed in trees and spent the night by a nearby stream. Two days later he was found by villagers who took him to their village about two thirds up on the northern side of the Finesterre Ranges. They escorted him to Saidor, where he was turned over to some Australians who paid them a reward for bringing him in.

Meanwhile, Anderson was flying his brand new "194" named *Virginia Marie*:

> After recovering from the spiral, I tried to get the Lightning straightened out and on some sort of a course. Needle, ball, and airspeed. It took just a few seconds to become accustomed to those instruments, but those few seconds seemed like years. Pilots were finding it increasingly difficult to listen to their radios. Every second was crowded with often firm, sometimes panicky calls for homing from either Nadzab, Gusap or Saidor. (For example) "Hello Backwards, this is Possum 176. I need a homing. Over. Hello Possum 176, give us a long count. Over. Hello Backwards. This is Possum 176 . . . One, two, three, four, five, six, seven, eight, nine, ten . . . ten, nine, eight, seven, six, five, four, three, two, one . . . over. "Hello Possum 176. Fly 148. Do you understand -"

> I struck out blindly through the murk on this compass course, hoping that when I arrived over Nadzab the weather would be clear and I would be able to let down safely. I slowly worked my eyes around the instrument panel. I looked at the artificial horizon. It said my left wing was down, didn't it - I looked again. It did. I straightened up the wing. I made my acquaintance with the rate of climb indicator and then the altimeter. It was like finding old friends long forgotten. Finally, I had the procedure down pat and then another ugly situation arose. Where was I? The best answer I could think of was that I was obviously over the Finesterre Ranges somewhere to the northwest of Nadzab. I had to make a choice and do it quickly. I could fly back west and get out of the weather and circle near the mouth of the Markham Valley in hopes of a break in the weather, or I could fly north, let down over the Bismarck Sea and try to get into Saidor, or I could fly east and hope to let down over Huon Gulf and fly back to Lae on the coast. I chose the latter course. Saidor radio was jammed with emergency calls. There was nothing but swampland at the mouth of the Markham. Not exactly a healthy atmosphere. East it was. I started climbing to see if I could break out, but at 27,000 feet the weather was getting no thinner. I levelled off. It was fairly smooth. Both belly tanks had long since run dry and I was working on my outboard internal wing tanks. They went dry one after the other. My main tanks were lowering fast, even though I was at minimum cruise and had the mixture controls as far back as I could get them. I looked at my watch and did a little quick figuring. I had been

Lieutenant Carroll Anderson's 433rd FS P-38J *Virginia Marie* which he landed at Nadzab after getting lost in the weather at high altitude.

> out about six hours. That meant I had about enough gasoline for another two to two and a half hours. In theory I should have been near Huon Gulf if I had flown a proper course and had given myself enough time, but I wasn't sure. I decided to let down to 10,000 feet and if I weren't out of the soup by then, I would bale out and take my chances on floating or walking home. Lady luck was sitting on my shoulder, for as I let down at 500 feet per minute, I found the only hole in the weather I had seen for hours. A green valley was at its base. I rolled the P-38 on its back and let it go. I pulled out at 3,000 feet with Lae dead ahead about five miles, and Nadzab at my right about 20 miles away. The mountains were beginning to taper away into foothills at the point where the weather ended. It didn't take long to buzz the tower and peel off, a belly tank which I presumed had dropped clear earlier, flew off and exploded near the tower with a resounding roar. I landed. Once on the ground I found that I was the fifth plane in. My crew-chief wanted to know if we had been in a scrap. Hell no, I said, the entire Fifth is lost in weather. Sergeant Bill Howell's face turned whiter than mine.

As 433rd FS Lightnings slipped away and lost each other somewhere in the dark storm to try it alone, Lieutenants Louis "Lou" Longman, Austin Neely and Lewis Yarbrough, somewhere inland from the coastal village of Bogadjim, rolled away in tight spirals never to be seen again. In fact, Longman (flying his 89th mission), drove into the Finesterre Mountains at high altitude near Mongou Village at the western end of the Finisterre Range near the Shaggy Ridge Gap. From the wreckage, not discovered until 2009, it is clear his Lightning impacted at high speed, nose first, leaving just shattered wreckage.

LeRoy Ross flew into the storm with the rest of the 433rd FS:

> When we entered the front, the clouds were so dense I immediately lost sight of all other airplanes and became disorientated. I had unfortunately left both my gyro compass and artificial horizon uncaged, and then the aircraft began to stall. I pushed forward on the wheel which made the P-38 shudder, so I pulled back. This resulted in the same thing. I immediately decided to bale out. I reached up and took hold of the canopy release and with my hand still on the release I took another look at the needle and ball. They were centred and the airspeed was normal, so I got back on the rudders and wheel and began to fly the airplane. The soup was so thick I could barely see my wingtips. I changed course for Nadzab and then openings appeared in the clouds. I looked to my right where another P-38 was flying my wing. I signalled for the pilot to take the lead but he refused. I later found out this was Lieutenant Howard Stiles who was even newer in the squadron than myself. I continued to fly the course which I had selected, and Stiles stuck to my wing like glue. We tried letting down through some of the holes, only to find mountain tops, so we climbed back to a safer altitude. We flew like this for what seemed like hours and after I said a prayer (Let There be Light), we broke out over Lae. As Stiles was about halfway down the runway one of his engines ran out of gas and quit. After counting our blessings and getting our planes refuelled, we proceeded to Nadzab.

Other 433rd FS pilots also found their way back. Lieutenant Schoener, mostly by instinct as he would later claim, eventually found his way to Nadzab. So did Lieutenant Pomplun. Lieutenant Joe Price's "182" remained in trouble somewhere along the coastline, and his radio interjections asked Saidor for homing directions.

Meanwhile Lieutenant Jack Daly found a gap near Dumpu, snuck through and landed at Nadzab. Jack Purdy, who had been flying on Kimball's wing, lost sight of Kimball upon entering the weather. He then swiftly turned back, descended rapidly, and followed the Markham Valley at tree-top height back to Nadzab. Purdy was among the first Lightnings to return there, logging only five hours for the mission. Captain Kimball found his way back there too. On the ground he admitted that he had not dared to fly on instruments but instead latched onto the wing of a B-25. It got him home just fine, but Kimball never did find out who it was so he could thank him.

Water Collision

After separating from the remainder of the 433rd FS early due to Wire's fuel problem, Wire and Ryerson climbed to 12,000 feet between solid overcasts of upper and lower cloud. They had no problems until they arrived just south of Madang where another solid wall greeted them. Wire had flown several missions in the area and knew from experience and despite the information on topographical charts, that parts of the Finesterres exceeded 14,000 feet. He led Ryerson up to 20,000 feet looking for a break, but had no luck. They then turned north and descended back to 12,000 feet. Here again they flew along the wall of cloud. Wire recalled:

> As we were heading back east, I saw a plane on our left so we headed for it. There it was, a nice big B-24 heading home. I called Mort and said "we hit it lucky, this guy

> has a co-pilot, a navigator and a radioman - let's latch on and follow him home" - we snuggled in close on his right wing. He rocked his wings to let us know we were welcome and then headed through that awful wall of clouds. We kept tucked in for about ten to fifteen minutes, when all of a sudden the B-24 went into a sharp left turn. I told Mort to hang on and climb and then we made a 180 degree turn and headed out. It took about ten minutes for us to settle down, and about this time, along comes a full squadron of B-25s. Again we tucked in on the right wing of the rear B-25. After about five minutes the whole squadron went every which way, and again we went straight up and into a 180-degree turn, and back out. After we were out of the worst of it I called Mort and told him that usually along the coast, when the weather came in, the clouds would rise a bit as they approached land, and leave a space we could fly in and still see what was ahead. He said - "OK, let's give it a try".

The two negotiated the stormy coast, very low, trying to glimpse landmarks. The conditions were vertiginous and at times it was difficult to make out the horizon above the waves which were working hard at moving up and down. Their forward vision was nil so both lowered their side windows to keep each other and the coast in sight. The two Lightnings, now dangerously low, had too much forward momentum to avoid an unexpected obstacle. Wire's starboard propeller clipped a palm tree which started vibrating the engine, so he feathered it. Down to one engine, Wire became tense and in his own words, downright scared. Ryerson, who had considerable instrument experience, radioed Wire he had had enough, and would climb out on instruments. Wire wished him luck and Ryerson's Lightning disappeared upwards into the murk. Ryerson later found Northrup, and both pilots later landed at Saidor, although Northrup bent his nose wheel in doing so.

Left alone, Wire concentrated on controlling his skewing Lockheed. He had no idea where he was, except he figured that sooner or later he would find Lae. Visibility improved. A small airfield came into view around which there was aircraft movement: he had found Yamai, the small army field used for L-4 Cub aircraft. Wire quickly swung right and configured his crippled Lockheed for a single engine landing. The field's small length meant that the touch-down point was critical. Wire was wide on the approach, however, and gunned the good engine to take him seaside for another attempt:

> When I got out far enough so I could just see the field, I headed south down the coast. As I did the clouds came down forcing me lower and lower. All of a sudden, I saw a wave that seemed to be higher than my wing. I hauled back on the stick, but too late. I hit the top of the wave. Hitting the wave bounced me up a bit and the nose started going down. I pulled back on the stick to level out and it came all way back into my lap. I knew then I had lost control. I leaned back and locked my shoulder straps, cut the mixture control off, and dumped the canopy. All this took very little time, but it felt like I was in a vertical dive. The P-38 handles well at 220 miles per hour indicated and this was what I had been flying at the time.
>
> I cannot remember hitting the water. I couldn't see it coming, nor feel it, nor hear it. All I know is I regained consciousness feeling as though I had needles in my ears. I unfastened my seat belt and kicked out of the plane. My clothes and parachute had

> enough air in them to float me to the surface. All I could think of was getting my life raft out. It took me some time and struggling to do so. I was getting tired of trying to stay above water. Then I thought, you fool, you have a Mae West on. I pulled the string and it inflated and I laid back for a bit of a rest. I finally got my life raft out and inflated it. This will show you how stupid or shocked I was - here I was in the sea with strong and awful waves, trying to get into that raft over the big end. I finally figured it out and turned it around and climbed in. It was full of water, so I spent the next fifteen to twenty minutes bailing it out. That was another mistake, with the water out it rode high like a big piece of balsa wood. The wind blew my raft around like a balloon, but it didn't take long to push the small end underwater and fill it so that it would ride better. I think I crashed about a half-mile off the coast. All went well after I got the water in the raft. The wind in the meantime was pushing me toward the shore. I could see a line of huge breakers ahead of me crashing over a reef and into the bay. This gave me another fright, but I must have been on the crest of a wave and it carried me over the reef and into the bay and much smoother waters. Coming toward me from the shore was what looked like a native dugout canoe with two men. Both of them were wearing some kind of conical hats. I immediately thought they were Japanese. I got my .45 out and tried to shoot at them. Luckily the gun wouldn't fire. They were GIs and towed me to shore. We had to wait at the landing strip for aircraft to crash land on the strip before we could cross. They took me to their first aid station and made temporary repairs to my face. I had torn off the bridge of my nose, and had a large cut on my forehead, in over my eyebrows, and my front teeth had been driven through my lip. The next day they sent me by LST to Saidor, and then by plane to an army hospital in Sydney. They kept me there for about four months for plastic surgery and R&R, then back to Biak in August 1944.

Clover Squadron Lose Two

Meanwhile the 432nd FS ("Clover Squadron") had dispatched two separate flights to Hollandia. The first of four accompanied the F-7s on their photographic assignment. It was from this flight that Lieutenant Robert Hubner developed mechanical problems over the target, and pulled away at 1330 to return home early, accompanied by Lieutenant Jack Luddington. Half an hour later the remaining two turned back with the F-7As, later leaving them at Burui at 1440 to find their own way home. The 432nd FS diary recorded:

> This second flight of Clover planes also ran into the front which practically obliterated their vision. Captain Loisel tried to keep the squadron intact by radio instructions, but the fear of colliding in mid-air caused many of the pilots to become separated. At this point, Captain Loisel had radio contact with Lieutenant Hubner. He was extremely nervous and in no condition to fly on instruments, so Captain Loisel advised him to bale out. Later Captain Art Peregoy heard Lieutenant Hubner talking to "Harvest" [Finschhafen] and that was the last that was heard of him . . .

Hubner's last transmission advised that both he and Luddington were together somewhere in the upper Ramu Valley, approximately 60 miles southwest of Madang. Both Hubner and Luddington (from Ogden, Utah), simply disappeared. Meanwhile the second and larger

Circled are *Satan's Angels* P-38 pilots Captain Art Peregoy (left) and Lieutenant John Parkansky. On Black Sunday Peregoy led a group of 432nd FS P-38s safely to Saidor.

432nd FS contingent of a dozen Lightnings led by Captain John Loisel had covered the *Roarin' 20s* A-20Gs but had been reduced to eleven Lightnings after Hannan broke away early, feeling ill. He was followed by another two aborts, leaving nine Lightnings to face the front. Loisel, a softly spoken Nebraskan who had orientated many new pilots into the Lightning, kept this contingent together until the A-20Gs started circling near the Gogol River, at the storm's face. Following Loisel was Lieutenant Dale Burgess:

> In hope of getting over the top of the front we dropped our external fuel tanks and then climbed to almost 20,000 feet, but the front was higher so we descended to about 11,000 feet where we no longer needed to use oxygen. Most of us were milling around in a fair-sized hole in the storm. Loisel contacted a controller who obtained a fix on our location and gave us a heading to reach Nadzab. The controller was asked if we would clear the 12,000-foot mountains at our present altitude and he replied, "I guess you should". Loisel replied that the controller had better be sure and not guessing. I then discovered that my artificial horizon was not functioning and I would have to fly needle, ball and airspeed. I told my element leader Cliff Mann what the problem was and that I would try to fly his wing. I tucked in as close as I dared and part of the time I could not see him because the cloud was so thick. Eventually we broke into the open not far from Nadzab. We chopped the throttles and headed down for home base. I was never so glad to be on the ground before or since.

From the larger 432nd FS contingent, several made it through to Nadzab just before dark while others landed at Saidor. Overall, the squadron lost two Lightnings, as referred to above (Hubner and Luddington).

MacDonald Disappears and two POWs executed

The 475th FG (*Satan's Angels*) became the first Fifth Air Force fighter group which was fully P-38-equipped. Comprising three fighter squadrons of the 431st, 432nd and 433rd FS, it had been activated on 14 May 1943 with both fanfare and subsequent publicity. It became the most famous of all the Fifth Air Force Lightning units, however on this critical day the group would suffer disproportionately. In the confusion some P-38 squadrons became mixed up and untangling the resultant mess at a distance is challenging. The group's official history summarises that:

> In the minds of some, weather had almost achieved the status of personality, the incarnation of a tricky adversary to be fought with caution and respect.

After reaching the front south of the Sepik River, a mixed formation of ten Lightnings made repeated attempts to penetrate the front while circling Astrolabe Bay. From the thick radio chatter, 433rd FS Operations Officer Captain William O'Brien assessed that getting back through the Markham Valley would not work. Keeping his group together instead he throttled back and guided them low along the coastline. Tucked in tight, the aircraft kept formation, exercising particular care in the frequent cloudbursts. Once reaching Saidor, they landed as soon as possible. Lieutenant Warren Cortner was among them, pleased they had all put down without a scratch. After parking their fighters, they sat on the wings and witnessed the unfolding crashes.

At this juncture it is worth recounting that only two months prior on 11 February 1944 the entire 475th FG escorted B-24s to Kavieng thus completing the longest over-water flight by fighters in the theatre to date. More escort missions to Kavieng ensued, gifting the pilots the experience of long-distance flights over water. The 431st and 433rd FS moved to Finschhafen on 26 February 1944, whilst group headquarters and the 432nd FS remained at Dobodura until 24 March 1944. Thus, the first two squadrons had become used to operating together. On Black Sunday, in the end, several flights from these squadrons became intermingled and reformed when searching for a way home.

At the edge of the front one 431st FS Lightning flown by Lieutenant Milton MacDonald, likely formed up with two 433rd FS pilots, Lieutenants Austin Neely and Louis Longman. At any rate, all were last seen five miles west of the coastal village of Bogadjim in thick cloud. The three went MIA, however through post-war discoveries their fates can be presented. Post-war identification of Longman's fighter ascertained it drove into the western end of the Finesterre Mountains near Shaggy Ridge Gap. Longman was flying the aircraft when it hit, was identified in 2013, and buried with military honors in Clinton, Iowa, the following year. The leaves the fates of Austin Neely and Milton MacDonald to be revealed.

In mid-1945 a Captain Hill of the 18th Australian War Graves Unit recovered the bodies of two US airmen from a grave near Amron. In December 1945 an Australian police lieutenant at Madang, William MacRae, interviewed local villagers who had been witness to the execution of these airmen. It is clear these were MacDonald and Neely, identifiable from physical descriptions given of both captives, and the timing of their capture given as a Sunday in April 1944. It appears that MacDonald and Neely, although from different squadrons, might have joined up after Longman separated from Neely; perhaps they agreed by radio to bale out together.

Regardless, the wreckage of their Lightnings is not far apart. MacDonald's lies not far from the village of Efu, and Neely's lies in the same vicinity. Both parachuted and were captured that Sunday afternoon. First detained was Neely, found near Amron by a party of Japanese-appointed native policemen. Kaut, the Japanese-appointed captain assaulted Neely when he resisted arrest and confiscated a gold ring from Neely in the process. This was returned to Australian police at the interrogation in 1945. Not far away, MacDonald meanwhile was captured near Efu village and brought to Amron later that same afternoon. Next afternoon the Japanese dug a slit trench outside the Japanese post at Amron as a grave. Each POW was forced to kneel at either end before they were executed by sword. The executions were supervised by a *Kempetai* Lieutenant Yosoka whose superiors were absent visiting Hansa Bay at the time.

Taken in early April 1944 at Nadzab are several 475th FG pilots who participated in Black Sunday. Left to right: Lieutenants Robert Tomberg (baled out), Austin Neeley (captured), Herbert Cochran, Lewis Longman (MIA), William Grady and Clarence "CJ" Rieman.

Captain Cornelius "Corky" Smith of the 80th FS with the new P-38J *Corky IV* he flew on the Black Sunday mission at Nadzab on 4 May 1944. Part of the 8th FG, the 80th FS suffered only one P-38 loss on Black Sunday. In comparison losses by the 475th FG were heavy, with the group's three squadrons losing ten Lightnings.

CHAPTER 7

SAIDOR "A HEART-BREAKING SIGHT"

We now turn to the carnage visited upon Saidor airfield as fuel-starved aircraft vied for landing. Resting obliquely to the coast, the airfield had been recently graded as a support airstrip and logistics base, complemented by nearby naval facilities. The strip sloped downhill slightly towards a jetty at its eastern end and rested at the foot of the Finesterre Mountains. Its surface was laid with Pierced Steel Planking (PSP), covering a freshly graded muddy base. Rough on tyres, PSP was particularly slippery in wet weather, and hard landings also had the ability to tear it up, producing a hazard for following aircraft. For the uninitiated, taxiing on its surface produced a loud noise, sufficient to defray already tense nerves. Halfway down the southern side was a rudimentary control tower, and just to its left, a limited parking area. Interconnected hardstand revetments lay both north and south of the airfield, but access to them was limited by taxiways exiting the strip's middle and northern areas.

The airfield had been operational just a few weeks. Based there already were the 58th and 348th Fighter Groups equipped with P-47D Thunderbolts, and two *Sky Lancer* A-20G squadrons. The 58th FG was not regarded as combat-ready, so for the present was relegated to escort duties and patrols. The 418th NFS also had a forward detachment of two P-70s (the night-fighter version of the A-20) based at Saidor from 1 April which was conducting night patrols from Cape Croisilles to Kar Kar Island. Then on 5 April the 421st NFS sent a detachment of six P-70s to Saidor as well. Although in Fifth Air Force terms Saidor was a comparative backwater, these forward-based units and detachments filled all available hardstand areas. The strip's limited length meant it was off-limits for larger bombers, at least that was the plan, but for two hours this late Sunday afternoon it became the southern hemisphere's busiest airfield. Around Saidor there was still limited enemy ground activity. Although the US 32nd Infantry Division, in conjunction with Australian forces, had occupied Saidor in early January 1944, pockets of desperate and hungry stragglers still roamed the surrounding jungle from the 78th and 239th Regiments of General Adachi Hatazo's 18th Army.

The first aerial activity at Saidor occurred mid-morning at 0945 when four 58th FG Thunderbolts scrambled in response to a false alarm. They scoured the coastal area for an hour and a half, found nothing, and were back on the ground at 1130. Saidor was quiet and overcast, the two *Sky Lancer* A-20G Squadrons having departed for the mission during their absence. A chapel service occupied the more pious that morning.

The Beginning of Chaos

Chuck Miles and three other 58th FG armourers were meanwhile aboard a navy barge delivering freshly baked bread to a 32nd Infantry Division contingent based at Yamai airfield, approximately five miles west along the coast. Miles later recorded:

> The afternoon found us away from shore, chugging along in the LCT, heading back towards Saidor. The weather was rainy - not stormy. The sky was extremely dark and ominous - completely socked in. Visibility at ground level may have been a couple of miles, but with any altitude at all, visibility must have been zero. We heard many, many different types of planes, flying in all directions, obviously lost and looking for a way down. We heard much more than we saw.

In constant succession aircraft materialised from the gloom, and it was soon evident that Saidor had a full-scale emergency on its hands. Personnel gravitated to the radio in the Operations Hut, adjacent to the south side of the strip, where they could hear the despairing calls of those lost. The 56th Fighter Control Squadron had activated its homing apparatus, a direction-finding transmitter with limited range, manned by Corporal John Kappastatter. Try as he might, Kappastatter's efforts were mostly futile. Atmospheric conditions, too static for accurate radio fixes, were also hampered by the fact that most aircraft were at low altitude, thus further impeding reception. Furthermore, agreed operational radio frequencies became hopelessly cluttered with pleas for help. Some appeals were ludicrous, some wretched and, towards the end, profane. The faster Mitchells were the first to arrive in the circuit area. *Sun Setter* 71st BS Mitchell *Seven Day Leave*, piloted by Lieutenant Paul Popma, was among them:

> The strip was wet and slippery. We landed quite fast as there was turbulence from other planes. When we came to a halt the right engine stopped. The navigator got out of the bottom hatch and walked forward under the wing first just as I was restarting the engine. He was hit slightly by the prop but not hurt.

Lieutenant Philpitt, flying *Sweet Jeanne* from the 71st BS, followed close behind. He made a tight circuit then landed long in heavy rain. Still rolling, his navigator threw open the top hatch to peer forward, then hollered to Philpitt that a Liberator was careering towards them. Philpitt immediately ground-looped, blew both main tyres and skidded the aircraft off the runway to the right. This action managed to avoid the oncoming Liberator as it skewed past. Rolling towards the runway's end behind them, *Sweet Jeanne* drove head-long into Lieutenant Popma's B-25, badly damaging both. Shaken crew scrambled out, then stood on the side watching disorder unfold as the circuit area thickened with aircraft. The co-pilot of *Sweet Jeanne* was Lieutenant Douglas Raaka:

> There was nothing much a person could do under the circumstances except stay out of the way of crashing aircraft.

Philpitt recorded the day as the worst carnage he ever saw, and now four more *Sun Setter* Mitchells were about to be destroyed in quick succession. While Philpitt and Popma's crew were scrambling clear of their wrecks, one from the 823rd BS broke through the rain about halfway down the strip. It started to slide, then just as its pilot Lieutenant Harvey briefly looked like he might regain control of *Old War Horse* it glanced off a dirt embankment, wrenching the main gears sideways. The Mitchell collapsed on both wing and belly, and although the crew got out without a scratch, *Old War Horse* had just made its last flight. An 823rd BS B-25H Mitchell named *GI Watch* blew a tyre on landing too, but otherwise was unscathed.

Colonel "GG" Atkinson, the 58th FG commander, was returning from Nadzab in his P-47D that afternoon where he had attended a meeting at Fifth Fighter Command headquarters. When he turned onto base leg two B-24s cut him out of the pattern, landing no more than about 600 feet apart. Atkinson touched down right behind them and burned off the tread of his tyres to stop running into the tail of the B-24 directly ahead. As he turned into the taxiway, he saw two other aircraft on short finals. As the senior commander at the airfield, Atkinson was designated "Airstrip Commander", responsible for refuelling units, the control tower and fire trucks: in summary all of the service units. He ran from his parked Thunderbolt to the control tower intending to take command of the worsening situation. Just as he arrived the blast from a head-on collision shook the area, the most serious of the entire day.

Runway Collision

In command of one of the 405th BS Mitchells was Lieutenant Robert Huhn, who like many others, was trying for Saidor in the poor visibility. In the circuit area were also two 26th PRS F-5A reconnaissance Lightnings (callsign "Topmost"), flown by Lieutenant Donald Christians and Captain Orville Counselman (the deputy commander of the 26th PRS). Both of these Nadzab-based Lightnings were also low on fuel when Christians touched down at Saidor's opposite end. His eight-ton Lightning and Huhn's Mitchell then collided head-on about halfway down the strip.

The resultant shattered wreckage burned fiercely, cooking off the Mitchell's 0.50-inch calibre ammunition. A 500-pound bomb which had hung up lay on the PSP outside the flames. The sight of mangled and burned bodies was horrifying. For those aircraft trying to land, the strip was now unusable. The tangled mess continued to burn, making it difficult to clear debris. The Operations Officer for the 58th FG, Major Harry Odren, shouted to bystanders to move in to try clear the debris. A survivor staggered out of the flames. Colonel Atkinson recalled:

> Running to the wreckage I could see that one crew member was alive but unable to get out. I had pulled on my leather gloves while running - I had a group policy that all pilots wear gloves while flying in event of cockpit fire - four of us arrived at the burning B-25 about the same time. The canopy, wind shield and side windows were gone, and we could see the crewmember pinned in the wreckage. I lifted some wreckage and the other three were able to lift him out. When I let go, the gloves fell off the back of my hands. After we got him into an ambulance, I discovered that one wing of the B-25 had been sheared off and was partially blocking the runway. We four grabbed the wingtip and dragged it off the side. The next morning, we same four attempted but were unable to lift the wing, much less move it. Strange how emergencies can motivate you.

Ground crews took winches to drag pieces of the burning mess. Part of a burnt corpse slid out from under the Mitchell wreckage. Someone else pulled out another crewmember, alive but also badly burned. Both these survivors would later die in Saidor Hospital: radio operator Lieutenant Frederick Rogers the next day and bombardier Technical Sergeant Joseph Carroll on 25 April. Huhn and his co-pilot Lieutenant William Barron were cremated beyond recognition, as was Christians the F-5A pilot.

While the burning wreckage was being cleared, Lightning pilot Joe Price made a straight-in approach, ignoring the flaming obstacle and destroying his P-38 #182. The incident marked the only moment of spontaneity on that bleak afternoon. As Price's Lockheed lifted and cleared an oncoming B-25 the watching crowd of hundreds let out a cheer heard all over the airfield. Many swore the cry was heard all over New Guinea (Price's detailed account of his day appears in Appendix 1).

Lieutenant Colonel Milton Johnson, the 417th BG commander, had stayed behind for the mission. He raced to the control tower when his two returning A-20G squadrons were forced to circle waiting for wreckage to be cleared. Their radio chatter left no misunderstanding about their low fuel status. The first 675th BS A-20G (tail letter N) to land was flown by Lieutenant Duane Aamodt whose starboard wing impacted with a protruding piece of Mitchell wreckage, clipping off five feet. Next to land was Lieutenant Thomas Grimes (tail letter O) whose gunners had advised when leaving the target zone that a bomb had hung up, but Grimes eased down the runway safely.

Meanwhile, seeing that Saidor's only runway was rendered unusable, Captain Alfred Moser headed the rest of the 675th BS for Finschhafen.

The A-20Gs of the 672nd BS in Saidor's circuit faced the same challenge. They discussed whether to continue eastwards towards the Huon Peninsula, then up the Markham Valley to Nadzab, but some said their fuel couldn't make it. From the control tower, Johnson told them they could land safely through the gap in the runway wreckage. One by one their A-20Gs established a right-hand traffic pattern, landing with their main gears close to the edge of the airstrip. Among them was Lieutenant Arthur Gresens flying *In The Mood*:

> I was on cross-feed with one tank very, very low and the fuel warning light on. I circled - waited for my opportunity for an approach, set it down nice and smooth only to go into a skid on the metal runway and crashed thru the planes which had collided head-on in the middle on the runway. Fortunately, *In the Mood* did not catch the full impact, but ended up against an embankment just off the runway after the right-hand undercarriage had collapsed. The plane was washed out, but my gunner James Christenson and I were OK - just shook up. What a day.

Captain Edmund Fowler was flying *Tommy's Dixie Gal*:

> Our only chance to reach home was to follow the coastline. Soon, we spotted a small landing strip. I circled and on the second pass decided it was too short for my use. It was on the second pass that the ground personnel at the strip had formed an arrow pointing southeast. This was taken to mean that I had not overshot Saidor. I continued down the coastline, and by now my fuel gauges were showing red warning lights. I

> knew I had to land soon! Just down the coast, I caught a glimpse of an anchored boat. In a split second, I remembered taking off from Saidor and flying over an anchored boat. I looked up and sure enough there was a landing pattern of circling aircraft! I did not have enough fuel to join them, so I came straight in over the anchored boat and there was the Saidor strip in front of me. Upon landing, I touched my brakes promptly, and started a skid on the muddy metal strip. I let up on the brakes and my plane straightened out. Then more trouble! There was a burning aircraft on the strip being pushed off to the left by a bulldozer. I did not have enough room for my left wing to clear. I touched my breaks again, to create a skid and slid sideways past the burning wreckage to the end of the runway, a right turn and to my revetment. I was home! My crew chief, Doc Combs, was waiting there in the soaking rain, sitting on an ammunition box with his head in his hands. When I cut my engines at my revetment, Doc looked up and saw me. Might I say that it was quite a reunion.

Next, two more A-20Gs landed to the extreme left-hand side of the strip. The nose-wheel of the first tangled with the runway lights, throwing them back through the propeller and showering the runway with glass shards. The second burst its front tyre on wreckage. The front gear was wrenched backwards, and the aircraft skidded on its nose through the burning mass. Both crews emerged unscathed. A *Sun Setter* Mitchell flown by Lieutenant Hamilton followed. It blew a tyre and veered off the strip, but the aircraft would be repairable. Two more A-20Gs were followed by a lone Airacobra which bellied in. So did another 3rd BG A-20G right behind. P-47s belonging to the 348th FG were parked at the end of the runway, close to the turn-off. As the second A-20G came barrelling through, it collected Thunderbolt *Dirty Old Man*, which in turn spun into and damaged an adjacent Thunderbolt. When the A-20G came to rest, many hands clambered to free its pilot, unconscious in the twisted cockpit.

Major Milton Johnson, the commanding officer of the 417th BG who tried to coordinate the landings at Saidor from the control tower.

Lieutenant Jay Robbins, aboard F-7A *Rip Snorter* in the circuit area as navigator, watched an A-20G cut in front of two landing P-38s which was warned off by red flares. More *Sun Setter* Mitchells, A-20Gs and Lightnings put down, followed finally by *Rip Snorter* which landed eastwards. Its brakes locked, gashing the right tyre, but under high power the Liberator strained its way sluggishly to a hardstand. Another

Lieutenant Royce Harms' 20th CMS F-7A as it came to rest at Saidor.

A-20G *Powerful Katrinka* as she came to rest at Saidor. The commander of the 13th BS, Richard Walker, had his approach interrupted when his wingman flew underneath him on finals. Ambulances can be seen in the background.

F-7A appeared in the circuit area. With two engines flak damaged over Hollandia, pilot Royce Harms was unable to hold the wandering cripple steady on the slippery runway as it skewed sideways left, collapsing the maingears, and shuddering to rest against an embankment. One gunner was injured. Another airman, who had just exited from a nearby crack-up, was likely spared his life when the F-7A's snout drove into a muddy ditch into which he had just leapt.

The next to enter Saidor's circuit was a gaggle of 13th BS A-20Gs, led by Major Richard Walker in *Powerful Katrinka*:

> When we arrived at Saidor at first I thought I saw an ocean wave sweeping over the airfield. A wave of green would surge to the runway and then recede and surge again.

> What it was were hundreds of GIs in the rain wearing their olive drab rain ponchos rushing up to the runway to see what had happened to the last airplane that had landed, then rushing back a safe distance from the runway as the next one came in for a landing. My squadron looked for a place to land without getting tangled in the existing wreckage. It looked like it was possible to land on the right-hand side of the strip and so I lined up on that. As I approached, my wingman Lieutenant Linzemier flew under me and landed in front of me. We both hit the ground at the same time. There was torn-up PSP everywhere, so I blew both tyres immediately. My airplane skidded off the side of the shoulder and came to rest in the mud. The remainder of the squadron landed wherever they could, and all got down safely, but the airplanes were in shambles. We had been overwhelmed by a force far more formidable than ourselves.

Another 13th BS A-20G named *Honeybunch* collapsed its maingear as it drove through the runway debris. A *Satan's Angel* Lightning with Stanley Northrup at the controls narrowly avoided hitting an oncoming Liberator, by hitting one brake to skid sideways, collapsing the nose wheel and bending both propellers. By now a total of eleven wrecked aircraft lay around the strip's perimeter. Two A-20Gs lay flat at strip's end. In the middle of the runway a burning plot and strewn wreckage still marked the collision between the F-5A Lightning and Mitchell. Three more Mitchells lay crippled around the perimeter, as did Harms' bent F-7A Liberator. Northrup's Lightning rested on its nose, while Joe Price's which had skidded on its belly looked equally forlorn, resting on the edge of the far tree line and covered in mud. Men from the 69th Service Squadron worked non-stop to do what they could to clear wreckage and move aircraft until 2300, resuming early the next morning to salvage what they could from damaged airframes.

Two Gunners Drown

When Captain Alfred Moser decided to take his 675th BS A-20Gs to Finschhafen, he was accompanied by Lieutenants John Simmons, Robert Mitchell, George Young, Paul Lucas, Roy Andermann, Harold Kohart, Robert Hadlin and Michael Jovanovich. Andermann's A-20G still carried all its nose gun 0.50-inch calibre ammunition as the guns had failed over the target due to an electrical fault. Halfway down to Finschhafen Jovanovich's fuel warning lights glowed red, and he knew he could not make Finschhafen. He climbed to 1,500 feet and gave his gunners Sergeants Melvin Cope and Jack Barr the option of baling out or ditching with the aircraft. They chose to stay. The A-20G ditched in a medium swell at 1655, with both props feathered and the canopy unlatched for a quick exit. The aircraft put down about 35 miles west of Finschhafen, and stayed afloat for barely 45 seconds, giving Jovanovich just enough time to inflate his dinghy. When he scrambled back along the fuselage to wrench open the gunner's Perspex top hatch the bomber sank beneath him. Jovanovich was rescued by a PT boat which took him to Finschhafen that evening, but both gunners had gone.

Yamai - Six Destroyed

Approximately eight miles to the west of Saidor was a small dirt airstrip built for small L-4 Cub aircraft assigned to the 32nd Infantry Division, used for spotting and reconnaissance.

An L-4 Cub assigned to the 32nd Infantry Division is unloaded at Yamai in March 1944. Several much larger aircraft crash-landed at Yamai on Black Sunday.

The 672nd BS A-20G forced-landed at Yamai by Lieutenant Phillip Crow, from which parts are being salvaged a few days later.

Yamai's surface this Sunday was muddy from the persistent rain. Late that afternoon B-25D *Fer-De-Lance* entered Saidor's circuit at the height of the confusion, piloted by Lieutenant Victor Maturi and co-pilot Lieutenant G Grendahl. Following an urgent debate, they agreed to back-track to Yamai rather than risk putting down on Saidor's burning runway. The Mitchell's gear collapsed in the mud, slewing through kunai grass adjacent to the tree line. The crew were cut and bruised, and the wrecked *Fer-De-Lance* would never fly again. It was an original 408th BS Mitchell transferred to the 823rd BS in late January 1944 when its original owners converted to Liberators. At time of publication its wreckage still lay where it came to rest.

When Moser's 675th BS A-20Gs broke away into trail formation to head for Finschhafen, pilot Ed Davidson decided that his fuel wouldn't carry him that far, so he turned back to put down on Yamai's short surface. Similar to *Fer-de-Lance* it carved through the thick mud at 1645, snapping sideways and collapsing the left landing gear. Davidson, thrown forward into his harness, was badly bruised. Gunner Staff Sergeant Schaefer received a cut scalp, but the other gunner Staff Sergeant Rounds was uninjured. After safely exiting Davidson repeated his concern about what "old man Moser", the group commander, would have to say about the cost to the taxpayer.

Meanwhile two more A-20Gs started circling Yamai. These were Lieutenant Donald Dower and his wingman who had left the 13th BS earlier in the piece and had become temporarily lost. Both were critically short of fuel and made short approaches, into the short muddy strip which was equally unsympathetic. Both airframes were rendered unairworthy through structural damage. Finally, 672nd BS pilot Lieutenant Phillip Crow also put his unnamed A-20G into the muddy strip. After dusk, all these forced-landed aircrews boarded a navy barge which delivered them to Saidor wharf at 2100. Behind them on the side of Yamai's short strip lay the wrecks of one Mitchell and five A-20Gs. It had been a long day.

When the next day dawned, it was obvious that the weather which had scourged New Guinea's northern coast was clearing. Crowded radio traffic tried to locate missing aircraft and establish the identity of those which had out landed. General Kenney arrived at Nadzab that morning for an update, leaving General MacArthur at Port Moresby to finalise arrangements for the Hollandia landing with Vice Admiral Daniel Barbey. Kenney recorded:

> I had landed at Nadzab the afternoon of the 17th ... The situation was definitely improved over that of the day before, but we were still missing too many crews and airplanes. There were plenty of grim faces around Nadzab.

Some crews were lucky. The crew of *Sun Setter* Mitchell *Tokyo Sleeper* which had put down at Cape Gloucester slept the evening in comfort, billeted in makeshift bunks in the 1st Marine Division mess there. After landing they had been provided with generous quantities of cigarettes, doughnuts and coffee. The co-pilot Terrell remembered:

> We were camped down by the ocean, and it was swell. We stayed up until midnight talking about the narrow squeeze the day before. We rose and shone to the clear call of a bugle sounding Reveille. We folded our cots and had a good breakfast - cream o'wheat, fresh butter, omelette and coffee. At 0730 hrs a 60-piece Marine Corps band, all slicked up, held a parade and flag-raising ceremony in our honour. I felt little tremors go up and down my spine - it was excellent. We pre-flighted our ships, took off, buzzed the field and flew back to Nadzab.

The crew of Liberator *Sack Bound* which had received hospitality from an AA gun crew at Finschhafen, had woken up early to pull the engines through before departing. Unfortunately, when they started the first engine it blew over their new friends' tent. As *Sack Bound* taxied out, the AA crew could be seen lining up behind the departing bomber making impolite gestures. When the crew returned to their tents at Nadzab they found all their belongings heaped in a pile. There was nothing missing, but as they had been classified as missing from the previous day, orderlies had cleaned out the tents. When word had got around that they were on their way back everything was returned. In the Fifth's bivouac areas rumours were wild and rife about Black Sunday's losses, the most rampant of which was that whole squadrons of fighters had gone missing in the front.

Lieutenant Roger Sullivan had put his 43rd BG Liberator down successfully at Saidor and was thankful to have survived the day. The next day he had another problem however - he was not convinced that Saidor's runway was long enough and so paced the strip with his flight engineer Sergeant Ken Strepp. They were still not convinced, so Sullivan put most of his crew on a C-47 bound for Nadzab. After the Liberator was lightened, he, Strepp and his co-pilot eased the Liberator off and headed there too.

CHAPTER 8

DOWNED AIRCREW

Black Sunday had left a trail of scattered downed aircraft, many behind enemy lines, whose crews now awaited rescue. Included were five A-20Gs, four of them *Roarin' 20s* machines: *Benny's Baby* lay in a swamp northeast of Annenberg, *The Hell'n Pelican II* had bellied into a clearing near the Gogol River close to Amaimon village, the broken *Lady Constance* lay near the village of Wabusarik (not far from *The Hell'n Pelican II*) and *The Texan* had been ditched northeast of Bogadjim. Its crew would never be seen again, but for the present Smart and Music were considered alive and easy to recover.

The 3rd BG had only one A-20G down - *Joy Baby* - its crew relaxing on the beach near Tokain village next to their aircraft, blissfully unaware of their peril behind enemy lines. With advice from their pilots, two A-20 gunners had baled out from separate aircraft over the Ramu Valley. At least two *Satan's Angels* Lightning pilots were somewhere in jungle behind Madang, one possibly already captured. *Stingeroo*'s crew of five were floating in their life raft near Japanese-occupied Karkar Island. Robert Stone's Liberator crew of eleven had baled out over the Finesterre Mountains but had failed to locate each other in the steep jungle mountainsides below. Each was struggling to find a way to safety on his own.

Whilst the weather cleared in the few days after Black Sunday, rescue efforts would be badly curtailed on 19 and 20 April 1944 when ADVON was forced to cancel most searches and all aerial strikes in New Guinea due to a fresh onset of poor weather. All USAAF units contributed to the searches alongside several Boomerang fighters from No. 4 Squadron, RAAF, based at Gusap. Their pilots knew the New Guinea terrain intimately, having spent the past year spotting and scouting enemy infantry positions.

Sixteen-Day Ordeal

Neither Davidson nor McKenna had received a scratch when force-landing A-20G *The Hell'n Pelican II*. Davidson was fairly sure that they had put down behind Japanese lines, and following military regulations, his first task was to destroy the aircraft's radios. Early

Two Boomerang fighters of No. 4 Squadron, RAAF, seen in 1945. Used in the army co-operation role, several of these aircraft were used to search for missing aircrew after Black Sunday.

Sergeant Howard Hines (left) and Lieutenant Charles Davidson at Hollandia following Davidson's return to duty after spending sixteen days in the jungle. Hines became Davidson's regular gunner after Sergeant "Red" McKenna grounded himself following the forced landing of *The Hell'n Pelican II.*

the next morning they laid out their parachutes and, mindful of a likely Japanese presence, McKenna worked the electric rear turret, confirming that its rotation and guns were still functional. Instructions and a map arrived by air instructing them to make their way to the wreck of *Lady Constance*. The terrain proved impassable, and rain rendered their compass unusable, so they returned to their aircraft. Over the next few days they underwent a variety of hardships, including being strafed early one morning by enemy aircraft. Friendly aircraft appeared daily with messages, dropping at one stage letters from Davidson's wife, Thelma. Fortunately, Davidson and his gunner had an established friendship, forged through having flown often together. Davidson always carried a Bible on missions, and McKenna now put the good Book to good use, learning passages by heart to help pass time.

For five days they tried to clear a small strip, with the aid of Gusap-based 49th Fighter Group P-40Ns which dropped belly tanks to burn a clearing. Frequent rain negated their efforts, however. It looked as if the two men might have to stay at the crash site for weeks, at least until the rain subsided. Then, on 24 April the Australian 7th Division captured Madang, and it was decided that since the town was secured the men should float down the Gogol River. An L-5 dropped a suitable raft the next day, and they hacked their way through to the Gogol's riverbank by dusk that evening. It took five more days to reach the coastline, involving a series of misadventures with crocodiles, and misplaced airdrops. The unhappy time, rarely short of variety, culminated with an accidental walk through the site of a recently bombed corpse-ridden Japanese camp. On 1 May Davidson and McKenna paddled alongside the RAN store carrier HMAS *Matafele*. It took them to Madang, from where they were flown back to Gusap. Their journey of deliverance had taken sixteen days.

Mystery of *The Texan*

After Captain Frank Smart cleanly ditched *The Texan*, the credible assumption was that its crew soon reached the safety of the nearby shoreline to await rescue and camped the night there. However, subsequent searches by VP-34 PBYs proved fruitless. In what constitutes Black Sunday's greatest mystery, Smart and his gunner simply disappeared. Exactly a week later at Gusap, the group chaplain Father Clatus Snyder held a service to pray for their safety and deliverance, but to no end.

Swamp-Ridden *Benny's Baby*

Of all the downed crews who force-landed that night, pilot Lieutenant Glen Benskin and his gunner JJ Westerman from A-20G *Benny's Baby* were the furthest behind Japanese lines. After spending their first night restlessly fighting mosquitoes, Monday's dawning sky confirmed the seriousness of their plight. Their bent-nose A-20G squatted in thick kunai grass while a jungle canopy, a few hundred yards away, appeared to offer sanctuary from the sun. Not long into the morning Boomerang A46-149 flew over - the first friendly aircraft to appear - and dropped a note asking the men to walk to Nagrubu village. Instead, they decided to make a more modest move to the jungle's edge. Such was the thickness of the kunai grass and swampy terrain that the short journey took two days, however. Towards dusk on the second day, Benskin cut his knee with his machete. They decided to return to their aircraft.

Regular supplies were dropped to them there while they passed the next nine days under the shade of a parachute draped over the wing. P-40 Kittyhawks were despatched to drop instructions and a map directing them to a landing ground made nearby from igniting belly tanks. Dragging their inflated life raft down to the Ramu riverbank, the men then floated downstream naked, keeping their clothes and guns dry in the raft, before reaching the clearing about half a mile downstream. That night it rained heavily, and on 25 April an L-5 dropped supplies and instructions saying they would have to wait until the ground was sufficiently dry. The men camped in the clearing for four more days. Benskin's knee gave increasing pain, to the extent where he considered suicide, then on 29 April another L-5 dropped machetes with instructions to clear the growth at the clearing's east end, a task necessarily undertaken by Westerman. On 1 May, a 25th Liaison Squadron L-5A flown by Staff Sergeant Walter James put down with a spare wooden propeller, then refuelled his light aircraft from cans stowed in the cockpit. Benskin was then boarded. James recorded that the L-5A's wing dragged in eight-foot kunai grass on either side as he departed, using every foot of the 225-foot clearing. The L-5A returned to Gusap via Faita where it refuelled. James returned to the clearing from Gusap and collected Westerman that same afternoon. Benskin had contracted scrub typhus and malaria, causing him to lose 40 pounds of weight. At Gusap field hospital he was offered a whiskey:

> I was in a badly weakened condition. Of course, the booze really hit me, and in a haze I told the field doctor that he could amputate my leg if he wished. Fortunately, he was more level-headed than I was at the time.

Escape From *Lady Constance*

The two crew of A-20G *Lady Constance*, Gibbons and Rhodes, had put down near Wabusarik village. A pair of 433rd FS Lightnings were airborne at dawn the next morning searching for survivors, led by Lieutenant "CJ" Rieman, who had experienced a gloomy night. All three of his tentmates - Tomberg, Neely and Longman - were missing, spurring his fervour to locate downed airmen. The pair soon found *Lady Constance*, with Carroll Anderson on Rieman's wing:

> We came across an A-20 where it had bellied in. The pilot's arm was in a sling. From the gymnastics of both men, it was apparent that our P-38Js were the first Allied aircraft they had seen since the day before. We flew back to Gusap and talked to a sergeant in *Guinea Short Lines*, and he was willing to fly up there with fighter cover.

The sergeant was again Staff Sergeant Walter James. At 0800 two L-5As departed, led by James, with cover provided by Rieman and Anderson. When they approached the site Gibbons fired a flare to attract attention. James dropped medical supplies and rations, then briefly surveyed the area before the four returned to Gusap where he suggested that a grassy area not far from the downed A-20G, sufficiently cleared, would be suitable for a landing. Warhawks next dropped and strafed belly fuel tanks at the site, however the grass was too wet to burn properly. An Australian ground patrol had meanwhile been despatched from Musak village to locate the crew but was turned back due to the proximity of retreating Japanese infantry. That night was cold, preventing sleep for the stranded men. Plans to clear an airstrip at the proposed site proceeded. Early on morning of 18 April, James circled the area, took bearings, and made a map with instructions which he dropped to the downed crew explaining how to reach the prospective strip, about 4,000 yards away. Tall thick wet grass hampered their progress, taking them six hours to reach the site. James was back again next morning to drop machetes, food and dry blankets. Enclosed were instructions to cut a clearing of no less than 150 paces. If all went well *Guinea Short Lines* would return tomorrow.

A Guinea Short Lines L-5 of the 25th Liaison Squadron. These light aircraft were involved in several rescues after Black Sunday, although short landing strips often needed to be cleared.

Rain the next morning delayed the first retrieval flight, however at 1330 Technical Sergeant Allen Lockwood put down. The field was not as good as he expected, the ground softer and the grass taller than it appeared from the air. He found Gibbons injured, and both men were hungry, wet and worried about proximity of the Japanese. Lockwood assessed a rescue departure feasible, and tried one, first with Rhodes aboard. The Stinson ran into tall grass at the end however, so all three spent the day's remainder slashing grass. That evening they cooked dinner on a shovel and tried to sleep in pouring rain. A clear dawn found them again attacking the wet grass. The ground had become softer, so they waited for the mid-afternoon sun to dry the ground before attempting another take-off, undertaken at 1530. Lockwood first attempted a take-off without passenger to test the strip. It worked, and Gibbons boarded for another attempt. Lockwood waited for the wind to come up and climbed out by banking between trees. He returned to Gusap around dusk, leaving Rhodes spending the night alone back at the clearing. James reappeared early next morning, but before take-off the pair cut down the trees which had nearly caused grief the previous day. Escaping *Lady Constance* had taken Gibbons five days and Rhodes six.

More Rescues

Upon advice from their pilots, two *Roarin' 20s* gunners, Sergeants James Revis and Stewart Down, had baled out over the wide expanse of the Ramu Valley north of Faita. Revis who had been flying with Lieutenant Walter Brooks broke his leg when he baled out. He was located from the air the next morning, and an Australian patrol was despatched to collect him. They became disorientated, however, and returned to Faita after their rations were depleted. In considerable pain, Revis was finally returned to Faita thence Gusap on 25 April. Similarly, Down, as previously related, had already been collected by an Australian patrol which returned him to Gusap on 20 April.

The five crew from B-25D *Stingeroo*, ditched by Lieutenant James MacWilliam, had spent Sunday night drifting in continuous rain. When the sky dawned, the current had carried them closer to Japanese-occupied Karkar Island, so they tried to paddle away. The air was thick with searching aircraft, but none noticed them until around midday when a flight of three Saidor-based Thunderbolts waggled their wings in recognition. The RAAF proffered their slow but reliable Walrus single-engined seaplanes, whilst VP-34 launched PBY-5s, including Blackcat #73, flown by Lieutenant James Merritt which landed around 1300 near the dinghy to collect MacWilliam's crew. With all aboard, the dinghy was sunk by the nose turret's twin machine guns to avoid distracting other rescuers. Merritt's PBY then headed for Billy Sanders and his gunner, relaxing beachside near A-20G *Joy Baby*. They had been located early that morning by four 36th FS P-38Hs, led by Lieutenant Orville Erdmann:

> We spotted an A-20 and men racing around on the beach. We called in to control and they said stay some distance away so as to not alert the Nips as to what was there. We did, and watched a Dumbo land later, taxi up near shore, pick up the men and depart very swiftly.

Sanders and his gunner were unaware that they were well-behind Japanese lines. This explains the nonchalance they showed when PBY-5 #73 taxied in to rescue them. The nose-gunner shouted to them to promptly board, but Sanders invited him to join them for a swim prior to departure. Just behind the beach was the Japanese road from Madang to the depot at Uligan Harbour. Prior to landing the Catalina crew had spotted Japanese soldiers approaching the crash-site, less than half a mile away. The gunner's precise response is unrecorded but was likely curt and blasphemous. An embellished account of the event soon reached General Kenney at Nadzab which raised several smiles. Subsequent to their safe extraction, P-40Ns from Gusap strafed *Joy Baby* and set it afire to keep it from enemy hands.

Those who had baled out from Lieutenant Stone's Liberator were meanwhile blindly stumbling their way through jungle in the lower reaches of the Finesterre Ranges, trying to find the other crew. For the present, however, the aircraft and its men were listed as missing. In the end two crew were never located, probable victims of exposure. At least two Lightning pilots were also wandering the jungles. Robert Tomberg, who had baled out, met friendly villagers on the Monday morning, and they soon guided him into Allied hands. Jack Luddington was either wandering in jungle or in Japanese hands; if not he would be within two days. Lieutenant Robert Keown had baled out over the Finesterres into a clearing, either killing him instantly or incurring injuries which hampered movement. Three A-20Gs were at Faita, one with a damaged nose wheel. Lieutenant Walter Bartlett walked Faita's muddy runway and decided it was long enough to take-off. He was soon taxiing *My Akin Back* at Gusap, where his crew chief greeted him with news that he had just been promoted to First Lieutenant.

At Gusap the following evening, the executive officer for the P-39Q equipped 110th TRS, Captain JR McClurkin, found himself on radio duty. Good news was still desperately short about missing aircrew, and when an important message arrived at 0200, McClurkin discovered he did not have the correct cipher. The message was eventually decoded, providing two pilots' names from another unit who had been declared missing but were instead safe at base. By now it was 0300, placing McClurkin in a dilemma. Orders were that all priority radio messages had to be delivered immediately to the commander, so he woke his commanding officer in his tent for a matter unrelated to his unit.

The *Roarin' 20s* commanding officer, Colonel Bob Strauss, held a wrap-up of the mission the following day during which he emphasised the importance of sticking with the group leader. He summarised matters by telling them if they broke off on their own, they had to accept full responsibility. Strauss also underlined that gunners should not be given the option of baling out. The pilot had to make command decisions for all crew aboard and was best placed to assess the dangers involved. The pilots later held their own post-mortem and were unanimous that such departures should not have been authorised.

On 22 April 1944, Operation *Reckless*, the invasion of Hollandia, proceeded as planned. Japanese resistance was light, and the area was soon secured.

A VP-34 PBY-5 is refuelled at Saidor in mid-1944. After Black Sunday one of these flying boats rescued five crew from the B-25D *Stingeroo* and two crew from A-20G *Joy Baby*.

The rescued crew of ditched B-25D *Stingeroo* at Nadzab after their ordeal. Left to right: Lieutenant James MacWilliam (pilot), Lieutenant Leo Fleniken (co-pilot), Technical Sergeant Robert Stewart (gunner) Staff Sergeant Jack Menefee (turret gunner) and Staff Sergeant Charles Sweet (engineer/gunner). Menefee long kept the paddle as a souvenir which Fleniken is holding in the photo.

CHAPTER 9

EPILOGUES

The airmen who survived Black Sunday would remember it for the rest of their lives. In the March/April 1944 aerial campaign against Hollandia, the Fifth Air Force dropped a total of 1,900 tons of bombs in a series of low, medium and high-level missions from 30 March through to Black Sunday.

Following the mission, many *Satan's Angels* survivors in particular had short life expectancies. 432nd FS pilot Henry Condon, whose Lightning made it into Nadzab at dusk, later became commander of the squadron, but was killed strafing a train on 2 January 1945 just north of Manila. A 432nd FS colleague, Lieutenant William O'Brien, who had slumped onto the wing of his Lightning at Saidor to watch the chaos unfold, lost his life in a head-on collision with a Tony fighter on 4 August 1944. Lieutenant Howard Stiles, whose engines had coughed dead from fuel exhaustion after landing, was last seen chasing an Oscar over Jefman Harbour in Dutch New Guinea on 16 June 1944. Another pilot, Lieutenant Mort Ryerson, was killed in a crash south of Dulag airfield in the Philippines on 6 December 1944.

Lieutenant Calvin Wire, whose Lightning hit a wave then ditched whilst flying on one engine, suffered serious facial injuries. The bridge of his nose was torn, there was a large cut to his forehead, and his front teeth were driven through his lip. He was medically evacuated to Sydney where he underwent four month's treatment including plastic surgery. He took some leave in the US, then later re-joined *Satan's Angels* in Biak in late 1944 where he finished his combat tour as a major. After his second tour of duty, he returned to the US to marry his childhood sweetheart Eva. Undecided what to do with his life, he took his brother's advice to become a fireman, a career from which he retired reaching the rank of Deputy State Fire Marshall.

Pilot "CJ" Rieman completed his second combat tour with 164 missions and two Japanese fighters to his credit. After the war he returned to his family business as a funeral director, from which he retired in 1970. Half a century later *Satan's Angels* pilot LeRoy Ross, who came within seconds of baling out, would forever attribute his survival to the exceptional stability of the P-38, with the assistance of the prayer *Let There be Light*, offered just before breaking out over Lae.

Lightning pilot Joe Price left the USAAF in October 1945. For the rest of his life, he too offered thanksgiving prayers for surviving the day. At the *Satan's Angels* 1984 reunion held in Scottsdale, Arizona, Dale Burgess met his former element leader Cliff Mann for the first time since the war. Burgess took opportunity to thank Mann for saving his life that fateful day, almost 40 years later to the day.

A thanksgiving service was held at the 1993 39th FS reunion at Colorado Springs conducted by the Reverend William Rogers, a P-47 pilot on Black Sunday. Former squadron commander Major Harris Denton and his wife were seated while Rogers recalled his time as a Second Lieutenant in the squadron, flying directly behind Denton in the Thunderbolt formation which had turned back. Rogers confessed he had been one of the more vocal in questioning Denton's judgment that day. Bill Rogers offered a public apology for all those young pilots who had bucked under the authority of Major Denton, saying that had they ventured to the other side of the front with their short-legged P-47s, it was almost certain lives would have been lost. The touching speech was accentuated by the common knowledge that Denton was dying of cancer.

A-20G pilot Andrew Weigel turned in his account of the mission at Nadzab after having led many stragglers safely back down the Ramu Valley. Almost a year later, on 13 March 1945, he was awarded the Distinguished Flying Cross for his efforts.

The day's event also became a landmark for Major Richard Walker, the 13th BS commander who led his A-20G squadron safely back along the coast to Saidor. The episode convinced him if he were to survive in aviation, he needed proficiency in instrument flying. Walker stayed on in the USAAF to command a Strategic Air Command B-47 squadron, before retiring with rank of Colonel in 1966.

Sergeant John McKenna, a 388th BS gunner aboard A-20G *The Hell'N Pelican II* who survived sixteen days in the jungle, became convinced that he would be killed if he ever flew again. The forced landing on Black Sunday marked his third aircraft crash of the war, and for weeks afterwards he related to his tent mates how he had been more scared of snakes than the Japanese. He grounded himself and was reassigned to ground duties. On 11 October 1944 he boarded a B-25D at Hollandia on a transport flight bound for Nadzab on his way home. Named *Five Minutes to Midnite*, the bomber remains missing.

The pilot of Liberator *Sack Bound*, Captain Erwin Zastrow, completed his tour and then returned to the US where he became a circuit court judge. In the 1980s he suffered a stroke and remained hospitalised for many years before finally passing away in the early 1990s.

Sergeant Lawrence Dickson, one of only three survivors of the 408th BS Liberator which crashed near Gusap after take-off from Nadzab, returned to the US for treatment of his lacerated leg. After the war he earned an accounting degree from the University of Kansas and went on to manage gas stations.

Whilst the day's tumultuous events escaped common knowledge for years, science-fiction author Robert Heinlein refers to "Black Sunday" in his novel "The Puppet Masters". The reference doubtless caused many fans to wonder what Heinlein meant, but Lightning pilot Carroll Anderson's son, Craig, confirmed with the author at a science-fiction convention in the 1970s that Heinlein indeed referred to Black Sunday.

Lieutenant Michael Jovanovich, the pilot who ditched his A-20G near Finschhafen, was later promoted to captain shortly after the *Sky Lancers'* move to Hollandia. There on 23 November 1944, Thanksgiving Day, the tyre on his A-20G blew on take-off, skidding the aircraft off the runway, and rolling the aircraft on its back where it caught fire. Two bombs then exploded killing all of the crew instantly.

Art Gresens, the 672nd BS pilot whose A-20G *In The Mood* was destroyed when landing at Saidor, returned to the US later that year. He became a drafting and design engineer, specialising in plant machinery.

John Hellstrom, the 2nd BS pilot who flew Liberator *The Lemon* was subsequently the sole survivor of a Liberator crash at Cairns, Australia, on 21 August 1944. Hellstrom would never fly with the military again, as associated arm injuries prevented a military career. He was medically discharged at Topeka, Kansas, in October 1945. On 19 August 1992 he passed away while practising as a lawyer in Davenport, Iowa.

The pilot of the only F-7A lost that day, broken up during its Saidor landing, was Lieutenant Royce Harms. He resumed his combat career, but on 30 September 1944 he and his crew lost their lives when their F-7B crashed near the Japanese-held airfield at Sarmi in Dutch New Guinea. In 1948 investigators ascertained that several crewmen had successfully baled out, of which at least two unidentified men had been executed by the Japanese.

The *Sky Lancers* 673rd BS did not fly on Black Sunday as it was still in the process of moving to Saidor from Dobodura and was equipped with early model short-range A-20Gs. On the morning after Black Sunday the squadron departed Dobodura for Saidor in flights of three but experienced a freak accident in the process. Flight leader Lieutenant Bernard Dotson commenced a series of shallow dives and turns once cruise had been reached, possibly to break the monotony of the long flight. During the manoeuvres conducted over the Huon Gulf, the canopy suddenly swung open releasing the dinghy stowed behind the pilot. It spread itself over the fuselage, disrupting the airflow and initiating a spiral dive to the left from which Dotson never recovered.

On Monday evening, 24 April 1944, a Catholic High Mass was celebrated at Gusap chapel by 312th BG chaplain Father Clatus Snyder for the temporal safety of missing crew of *The Texan*, Smart and Music. Black Sunday survivors who had since returned safely home occupied the front rows. The surviving pilot of *Lady Constance*, Joe Gibbons, acted as server during mass.

Weather took its toll on the enemy as well. On 21 April, the evening before the invasion of Hollandia, Admiral Koga Mineichi, the IJN regional commander, went missing aboard his G4M1 Betty bomber, which ditched during a storm north of the Halmaheras on its way to Davao. All aboard perished. His loss, monitored by Allied signals intelligence, rendered the Japanese leaderless during the invasion of Hollandia.

The last JAAF fighter mission in New Guinea occurred on the day after Black Sunday, 17 April 1944, when 77th *Sentai* pilot Sergeant Kumasaki Masashi conducted a maritime reconnaissance mission from Boram at 0310. He failed to sight any vessels.

Those participant Black Sunday aircraft which survived the war were scrapped at either Nadzab or Biak by the late 1940s.

Black Sunday left New Guinea littered with remote aircraft wrecks, several quite intact. A-20G *The Hell'n Pelican II* was salvaged by the RAAF in October 1984 after having been

Wing Commander Tom Kelly, RAAF, sits on the engine of *The Hell'n Pelican II* during its 1984 recovery.

located in heavy undergrowth by the author some eight years prior. Two other Black Sunday A-20Gs from the 312th Bombardment Group, *Benny's Baby* and *Lady Constance* were salvaged by the RAAF in 1985.

Mitchell *Fer-de-Lance* still lies on the side of the former US airfield at Yamai, its small yellow bomb mission markings still clearly visible but fading. An 89th BS mission participant, A-20G *Big Nig*, survived the day but was forced-landed the following month. It was recovered by the RAAF in 1995 and is now on display at the Pima Air & Space Museum as a restored exhibit.

Like any historical episode, myths have grown around the eventful day, the most glaring of which is the reference that Black Sunday fell on Easter Sunday. In fact, Easter Sunday 1944 fell on Sunday 9 April. Another myth is that the weather grounded all USAAF operations in New Guinea several days before the mission, thus adding weight to the claim it should not have been authorised. This is not the case; there were several successful large-scale missions against Tadji and targets along the northern New Guinea coast conducted the day before.

The closing comment about Black Sunday should refer to those lost men and machines still not yet located. The Fifth lost many aircraft during their Pacific war. After the war, both US and Australian search teams extensively searched New Guinea for missing Allied aircraft. Administratively, the "final" search of New Guinea was made by the US military in 1948. Searches were confined by the vastness and inaccessibility of New Guinea's geography. They still are, but some might be surprised to learn that at time of publication today the search continues. US citizen Justin Taylan, the founder of pacificwrecks.com, is currently engaged in ongoing research to locate missing US aircraft in New Guinea, including those missing from Black Sunday.

Since 16 April 1944 there has never been a weather-related aviation loss comparable to Black Sunday. Given modern avionics, there will never be. Total aircraft losses[1] were:

- Three aircraft abandoned mid-air (one B-24, two P-38s)
- 21 aircraft badly damaged or destroyed in operational accidents (ten A-20Gs, three F-7/ B-24s, three F-5/ P-38s and five B-25s)
- Four aircraft ditched (two A-20Gs, one P-38 and one B-25)
- Four aircraft force-landed away from base (four A-20Gs)
- Eleven aircraft missing (two B-24s, eight P-38s and one B-25)

Of the above eleven MIA aircraft, since the war either the wreckage or the fates of five P-38s and two B-24s have been determined. This means at time of publication there were still three P-38s and one B-25 missing.

A-20G Benny's Baby as it came to rest in a swamp. Note the swathe of long grass it has flattened in the process of landing gear-up, before spinning around.

1 The "losses" detailed here total 43 aircraft. However, a number of those damaged were later repaired. Further complicating matters, a few airframes were held for parts but were not formally written off until sometime later. Hence the precise definition of a write-off or loss can be problematic. Appendix III details the identities of 46 Black Sunday aircraft lost or damaged. The author has defined 37 of these as definite losses.

APPENDIX I

WHO KNEW IT WAS SUNDAY?

Years after his ordeal, *Satan's Angel* Lightning pilot Joe Price recorded his Black Sunday experience. Price graduated from Williams Field, Arizona, in Class 43-I and was ordered to report to Salinas, California, for P-38 training. Price was as surprised as he was delighted. After logging 100 hours in the type, he was assigned to the 475th FG, which he joined at Dobodura in February 1944. What follows is Price's account of the day exactly as he wrote it in his own descriptive and visceral style.

> Who knew it was Sunday - This was just another day in Nadzab, New Guinea. Hot as usual. Cloudy one minute - clear the next. Crew chiefs were pre-flighting the planes, jeeps running hither and yon, and pilots coming and going from the operations tent. The 433rd was to cover B-25s to Hollandia. There were three airfields there which had already been bombed incessantly with no aerial opposition since April 12th, but General MacArthur wanted it blasted one more time before ground troops moved in. We were all set. Then the mission was scrubbed - two or three times. Now, it was on again. This would be my twenty-eighth mission. I was Flying Chase Brenizer's plane #182. Sergeant Masengale was doing a 100-hour inspection on my #196.
>
> Hollandia was my nemesis, my Waterloo. This was our seventh flight up that valley. We had been on March 30th, 31st and April 3rd, 5th, 8th, 12th and now the 16th. One mission, flying high cover, 25,000 feet for B-24s, my oxygen mask tube came loose where it was snapped to my shirt. I did manage to get it back together before I went out and fell over the yoke. I came to at about 6,000 feet in a 70-degree dive with the throttles wide open. I had come down through all the B-24s as well as the Lightnings and Oscars who were really having a big dogfight below our squadron. Out of the blue, I heard Ken Ralph asking if I was OK. He knew something was wrong and had followed me. I said yes, I was going home. He answered "No, you're not. You're headed for Japan. Can you - will you follow me and please cut your throttles". I did. We made a big circle and went home. That was that mission except when Major Lewis came tearing at me, thinking I had broken formation to get in a scrap. I was still light-headed and nauseous. I lost my breakfast at his feet. I lost my electrical system one mission and flew 600 miles back with no radio or prop control. Fortunately, I made a good approach the first time and landed without problems. Next I was within 25 miles of the Cyclops Mountains, Hollandia, when I felt an attack of malaria coming on. I was hot. I had experienced this before. I called Possum Red One and told him. He called my element leader to go back with me. I told him there was nothing anybody could do - so I turned back alone. I soon began to really have trouble seeing. I called the tower for landing instructions. I told them I was now about 50 miles out, to make sure there was no other traffic, as I would be there in less than ten minutes. The tower came back, "there ain't a damn

thing wrong with that airplane". I said that it wasn't the plane, it was me, that I was burning up and if my vision got any worse I would just have to bale out. I did manage to get it on the ground, somehow. An ambulance was waiting. They dragged me up and out of the cockpit and on to the hospital.

So, what would happen today- The sun was shining when we finally lined up on the strip. Captain Dick Kimball, Red leader, rolled away and up. He was flying Major Lewis' (Possum Squadron CO) plane that day. It had red, white, and blue markings on the tail. The only plane that did. The fifteen of us followed and formed up. I was flying tail-end Charlie in Blue Flight. We headed up the Markham Valley. I already knew my radio reception was intermittent. I should have returned to Nadzab, but I didn't. I tucked in on Bob Anderson's wing. Shortly, we were over the B-25s. They were my favourite plane to cover. They were fast enough that we did very little weaving back and forth over them. Two hours out, we were approaching the flat land of the Sepik River country. The weather on our course had not changed much at all, but north to our right, I saw the thickest black wall of weather I had ever seen. It looked as if it exactly followed the coastline back southeast as far as I could see.

This was just another dry run. There was very little flak as the B-25s dropped their bombs. It gave us a good chance to look the place over and wonder which airfield Possum Squadron would be assigned when we moved up, which we knew would be soon. I couldn't hear much, but Captain Kimball was evidently not concerned about the weather. We engaged in a rat race in and around the B-25s doing slow rolls as a nose-thumbing gesture to the Japs. Then we formed up in a loose formation and headed home. Engines droned on. After about an hour I knew the others were getting concerned about the worsening weather due to the tightening of formation. I stayed right on Andy's wing. I wished I could hear something on my radio. Tinkering with it didn't help. Surely somebody was commenting on this mess. We were making our way in and around the edge of the front. It was getting a little rough. It became harder to see the ground. Suddenly, we were in the clouds and you couldn't. Evidently, Kimball made a sharp left turn to get back out into the clear. I was fighting my throttles to stay in formation and alive. Remember, I was in the rear and couldn't see anybody now. I don't know how many came back out of this together. Visibility was nil. I just hoped no planes had run together. I thought surely we were going to circle and think this thing over, maybe go down to the deck, see how it was down there, but instead, Captain Kimball led us back into that black mass of clouds. Disaster struck - here we are in tight formation - not fifteen feet apart in a zero visibility situation. None of us had any actual instrument experience. Couple this with the fact that we were low on fuel, over enemy territory and some high mountains. I was doing my best to stay in formation when all of a sudden, in just seconds, something caught my eye. A P-38 was right over me my head. I pushed my wheel forward as far as I could and gave it a big twist to the right! Probably the most uncoordinated diving turn of the war. I ran through the prop wash of another P-38. It was so violent that I thought I had collided with someone. I looked around my armour plate to see if my tail booms were still there. They looked OK, but my needle was in one corner and the ball in the other, and my speed approaching 400 mph. Every move I made to centre them was wrong. I knew I didn't have much time. I took my hands off the yoke, my feet off the rudder, undid my shoulder harness and reached for the emergency canopy release.

This was what I called an emergency. Just as I started to pull the release, I glanced at the panel. Good 'ole P-38. The needle and ball had centred themselves when I quit fooling around with the controls. Finally, I got pulled out of this screaming dive and shortly my airspeed went down to 80 mph. I had done a complete loop. It must have been a good one without the harness. I had sat tight in my seat all the way through. I milked it through a couple more dives and climbs, got it to a level altitude and a steady 200 mph cruise. It was nice to be able to reach up and uncage my Artificial Horizon without worrying about it being tumbled by the aerobatics I had been doing. The clouds were not nearly as thick at whatever altitude I'd leveled out at. But, where in the hell did everybody go - I was sitting there fat dumb and happy congratulating myself on being able to pull myself out of that mess on needle ball and airspeed, wondering where I was, when to my left there went a P-38 a few feet off my wing going straight up. It was clearly the ship being flown by Captain Kimball with the red, white and blue markings. Wait a minute - is he going straight up or straight and level and me going straight down - Oh God! I put my ear closer to the canopy to check for a build-up in wind noise, checked my airspeed again, my rate-of-climb indicator. I had to trust my instruments and just hope I wasn't about to build a big hole. I was lost. I was utterly confused, but I knew it. I hardly knew where Saidor was, but I did know it was on the coast. I could go over to the water and not have the mountains to worry about, like you would have getting to Nadzab.

"Cowpox", the code name for Saidor, popped into my mind. I tried to call them a couple of times. Nothing. It dawned on me that I hadn't heard anything on my radio. It was time for somebody else to get in on this thing. I said "OK, here we are. I don't know where we are or where we are headed. The radio doesn't work (I pointed my finger at the fuel gauges) and we are about out of fuel. If you want me to get home, I need help now". Believing He had heard me (I was talking out loud) I called Saidor again. I got a very faint response. I could barely hear. They ask me for a long count and to give my name. I answered Possum lost - and I do mean lost! They came right back and gave me a heading to Saidor, and said something about me baling out. I wasn't sure what they meant by that, but I could worry about that later. I kept watching my fuel gauges and changing tanks as they became empty. I ran on each tank until the engine it supplied came to an abrupt stop. This was another first for me - to do this on instruments. I began to hear more faint radio talk. It sounded as if the entire Fifth Air Force was in the Saidor area asking for headings. Suddenly I barely missed trees that were on a mountain top higher than my map showed. I gave full power and climbed to 18,000 feet before levelling off. At this altitude I could hear Saidor loud and clear. I could tell by the radio conversations that something bad had happened at the Saidor strip. When I next checked with the tower, they changed my course 60 degrees. I said, "My gosh, I'm running tanks dry- one after the other. I like don't have time for mistakes like this". Then I really became unnerved when I heard a pilot screaming, "I'm going in. I'm going in". I yelled into my mike, "Bale out, Bale out". There were a few seconds of complete radio silence. I tried to regain my wits. The next time I called Saidor, I said, "I'm surely over you now. What am I supposed to do -" Tower replied, "We still plan for you to bale out, but there's so much going on here, nobody would even see you. We have had a mid-strip collision of a P-38 and a B-25. We don't have a PT boat to pick you up. Go out over the water and circle. We'll stay in touch with you. They are clearing the wreckage now". I reminded him that I had run everything dry but my reserve tanks, and they were going fast. They said that they would have a PT boat in a matter of minutes now. I made my let-down, making sure I stayed out over the water at about 10,000 feet. I removed my oxygen mask and for some reason I looked down and was sure I could see the water straight under me. I still had no call, so I let down some more to see if I could get under this stuff with enough visibility to land on the strip while on the let-down. I slowed my airspeed to 130 mph and used one quarter flap setting. At about 200 feet it was raining hard. With the help of my gyro horizon I could level my wing and hold a heading if I could get one. I called in again and told them I had made a let-down and was in visible contact with the water. They gave me a heading, claimed they had been trying to call me and asked about my fuel. I told them I had just a few minutes left. Then they said they were ready. A PT boat was heading out on my course, to ditch at once.

Then for some reason, I informed him I was the one flying this damned airplane and would continue until the fuel decided differently. I think I heard a faint response. I believe the ceiling was 400 to 600 feet when I first saw the coastline. I told the tower I had to make a turn, now. He said, "Look over your right engine, Possum". I did, and immediately made a hard right turn with gear and flaps coming down. As I was flaring out with my left reserve tank showing empty and the one on the right moving slightly, I looked straight up the strip and saw a B-25 coming head on. I gave it full throttle and pulled gear-up, barely missing a head-on collision. I climbed to my right toward the water gaining all the altitude I could. While telling the tower I was going to have to ditch now, I couldn't make another pass, he asked if I could make a 180 and land back southeast. I said I didn't think so, but I would try. I started a steep turn for the northwest end of the strip. Then the tower started screaming at a landing B-25 (Everybody says it was a B-25, but I would swear they were calling it an A-20) that the P-38 on approach was completely out of gas. I couldn't see him under me until my left engine quit. With my right engine at full power and a very slow airspeed, it almost turned me over on my back. My left wing tip was almost in his cockpit. I stood on my right rudder and left power on my right engine until, I hoped, I had cleared the B-25. I landed a few feet ahead of him, wheels-up, and slid to the end of the wet metal strip. While sliding, I pulled my emergency canopy release, continuing to look at the B-25 in my combat mirror. I could tell that he was slowing faster than I was and that the canopy hadn't hit him. I had good rudder control until I slowed to about 70 mph. I then slid off in the mud with about three feet of my wing tip over the strip.

There were hundreds of GIs lining the strip watching the Fifth Air Force destroy itself. Everybody was screaming at me to get out before the plane caught fire. I hollered back, "There's no fuel. It can't burn. That's the reason I'm sitting here in the mud". Suddenly, I felt a sharp pain in my chest. I thought, Gosh, I've been shot, far-fetched as that was. Then it dawned on me that I had tightened my shoulder strap and belt in anticipation of a crash-landing. My .45 was imbedded in my chest. I reached for the holster, but came out with just the pistol, pointed toward the GIs. They began yelling and trampling over each other to get out of my way. I plainly heard one of them say, "Run, the son of a bitch has gone crazy". Some nice Colonel came over to the plane and complimented me on "the best flying he had ever seen". I remember he said, "You did lose an engine on your final turn, didn't you?" He extended his hand to help me out and in my anxiety I slapped it away which embarrasses me to this day. Needless to say, he left. I sat there in the rain trying to fill out my combat report (maybe I was crazy). I had logged seven hours fifteen minutes. By then my buddy, Mort Ryerson, got to the plane, said he had gotten in safely sometime. He told me that Northrup had had a minor accident with his nose-wheel when he braked trying to dodge a B-24, "Why don't you get out of that damn torn up thing and get out of this rain -" I proceeded to try, but when I stepped off the trailing edge of the wings my knees completely buckled and I fell flat on my face in the mud. Mort helped me up but that had really set me off. I threw my Mae West down and jumped on it. I pointed to my airplane and said, "Look at the damn thing, I've torn it all to hell". It had been a long day (I've read that I fell unconscious. Maybe I would have been better off if I had been.) Mort said he had found a place for the night, but he didn't know where anymore places were. Saidor was full. I took off walking in the rain. First things first - I needed to tell somebody to report back to Nadzab that I was safe so that my family would not hear that I was missing.

I walked up the strip, level with the tower at least a mile over, crossed over and looked up. There came a B-24 on final. Going up the tower steps, I heard someone say, "Here comes another one. Let's watch them crash". From his approach, I saw no reason for him to have any trouble. Then I heard, "There he goes". I looked and sure enough, he had ground-looped, probably due to over-braking. I believe that was the last aircraft to land on the Saidor strip that day. I went on in and conveyed my message to the tower. I don't know why in the world they let me in the tower with my .45 after the way they had screwed me up. Somehow, I ended up in the back end of a big high truck. It was now dark. They were taking me toward the hospital tent, but I would have to walk about 200 yards. When they told me to get out, I took one more step than there was truck, catching myself on my thumb, before I hit the ground again. I was sure it was broken. I got up and headed toward the dim lights of the hospital. I walked right into a water-filled foxhole. Would this day ever end - I found a cot. I must have just fallen in and slept in my wet clothes. I'm sure I didn't have any food either. It was a rather fitful night. The next morning when I opened my eyes, two Army lieutenants were sitting on a cot next to mine, staring at me, "We don't know what happened to you yesterday, but we're sure glad we weren't with you". I apologised for keeping them awake.

I found a ride on a B-25 back to Nadzab. I remember pointing out to the crew #182 lying there in the mud. You know how a crew chief feels about his airplane. I dreaded facing this man. When we landed, a sergeant drove me in a jeep over to the 475th tent. The first man I saw was him. I guess he had heard. Playfully, I took out my .45 and held it over his head, "Sergeant, I tore the hell out of your airplane yesterday and I am sorry". He grinned and said, "We can get another one". Then he put his arm around me. Hey, that was the only hug I got while I was in New Guinea. The longest day and night of my life was over, and I was 'home' again. Oh, I did thank Him".

A line up of P-38J-5 Lightnings on the 433rd FS flight line at Nadzab in February 1944. These early camouflaged "J" models lacked the extended range of the later natural metal finish models as flown on Black Sunday.

APPENDIX 2

PERSONNEL KILLED OR MISSING IN ACTION

NAME/ POSITION	GP/SQN	AIRCRAFT	STATUS
Anderson, S/Sgt Harold W, Gunner	345/ 500	B-25 #41-30315	MIA
Archer, Lt George E, Navigator	43/ 403	B-24 #42-72946	MIA
Barr, Sgt Jack T, Gunner/Observer	417/ 675	A-20G #43-9488	KIA
Barron, Lt William G, Bombardier	38/ 405	B-25 41-30337	KIA
Bettencourt, S/Sgt Lawrence	22/ 408	B-24 #42-109975	KIA
Bidgood, Lt Robert B, Co-Pilot	345/ 500	B-25 #41-30315	MIA
Borofsky, Sgt Marshall, Radio Op	22/ 408	B-24 #42-100225	MIA
Brick, Sgt Daniel L, Gunner	345/ 500	B-25 41-30315	MIA
Carroll, T/Sgt Joseph, Bombardier	38/ 405	B-25 41-30337	KIA
Christians, Lt Donald, Pilot	6/ 26	F-5A #42-67350	KIA
Cooley, Lt Raymond A, Pilot	43/ 403	B-24 #42-72946	MIA
Cope, S/Sgt Melvin G, Gunner	417/ 675	A-20G #43-9488	KIA
Fischer, Sgt Robert E	22/ 408	B-24 #42-109975	KIA
Franklin, Lt Harry C, Co-Pilot	22/ 408	B-24 #42-110000	MIA
Grady, Lt Donald F, Bombardier	43/ 403	B-24 #42-72946	MIA
Guigliano, Lt Frank P, Bombardier	22/ 408	B-24 #42-100225	MIA
Gullion, 1/Lt James P, Navigator	22/ 408	B-24 #42-100225	MIA
Halaby, Lt George J, Navigator	22/ 408	B-24 #42-109975	KIA
Harm, Sgt Walter G, Gunner	22/ 408	B-24 #42-100225	MIA
Hooper, Lt Edward E, Bombardier	345/ 500	B-25 #41-30315	MIA
Hubner, Lt Robert L, Pilot	475/ 432	P-38 #42-67594	MIA
Huhn, Lt Robert H, Pilot	38/ 405	B-25 #41-30337	KIA
Ives, Lt Dudley R, Co-Pilot	43/ 403	B-24 #42-72946	MIA
Jennings, Sgt Earle A	22/ 408	B-24 #42-109975	KIA
Kempkey, Lt August K	22/ 408	B-24 #42-109975	KIA
Keown, Lt Robert R, Pilot	8/ 36	P-38 #42-66668	MIA
King, S/Sgt Richard F, Radio Op	22/ 408	B-24 #42-100225	MIA
King, S/Sgt Joseph M, Gunner	43/ 403	B-24 #42-72946	MIA
Knight, S/Sgt Thomas G, Radio Op	43/ 403	B-24 #42-72946	MIA
Kravet, Lt Jules H, Co-pilot	22/ 408	B-24 #42-109975	KIA
Longman, Lt Louis L, Pilot	475/ 433	P-38 #42-104390	KIA
Lowery, S/Sgt William, Gunner	22/ 408	B-24 #42-100225	MIA
Luckenbach, S/Sgt Elgin J, Engineer	22/ 408	B-24 #42-100225	MIA

NAME/ POSITION	GP/SQN	AIRCRAFT	STATUS
Luddington, Lt Jack F, Pilot	475/ 432	P-38 #42-67605	MIA
MacDonald, Lt Milton A, Pilot	475/ 431	P-38 #42-104355	KIA (executed)
May, S/Sgt Marion B, Engineer	22/ 408	B-24 #42-100225	MIA
Mikucky, Lt Walter, Pilot	8/ 36	P-38 #42-66555	KIA
Murphy, Sgt William, Radio-Gunner	345/ 500	B-25 #41-30315	MIA
Music, T/Sgt Mike, Gunner	312/ 387	A-20G #43-9098	MIA
Neely, Lt Austin K, Pilot	475/ 433	P-38 #42-104385	KIA (executed)
Nell, S/Sgt Norman L, Engineer	43/ 403	B-24 #42-72946	MIA
Paschal, Capt Thomas C, Pilot	22/ 408	B-24 #42-100225	MIA
Picucci, Pfc Americo G, Engineer	22/ 408	B-24 #42-110000	MIA
Rayzor, Lt James F, Pilot	22/ 408	B-24 #42-109975	KIA
Reeves, 1/Lt Lawrence, Pilot	8/ 36	P-38 #42-66832	KIA
Rehmet, 2/Lt Leland A, Navigator	22/ 408	B-24 #42-100225	MIA
Rogers, Lt Frederick C, Radio Operator	38/ 405	B-25 #41-30337	KIA
Sargent, T/Sgt Richard R, Engineer	43/ 403	B-24 #42-72946	MIA
Smart, Captain Frank P, Pilot	312/ 387	A-20G #43-9098	MIA
Smith, S/Sgt Blair W, Gunner	43/ 403	B-24 #42-72946	MIA
Waggle, Lt James A, Pilot	345/ 500	B-25 #41-30315	MIA
Widsteen, 2/Lt John A, Co-pilot	22/ 408	B-24 #42-100225	MIA
Yarbrough, Lt Lewis M, Pilot	475/ 433	P-38 #42-104381	MIA
Zayac, T/Sgt Steve, Radio Operator	43/ 403	B-24 #42-72946	MIA

APPENDIX 3

AIRCRAFT LOST AND DAMAGED

1. A-20G serial 42-86563 13th BS/3rd BG, tail letter P

First to break formation from the returning 13th BS A-20Gs was *Joy Baby* (see Loss 12) that had both mechanical problems and was low on fuel. Lieutenant Donald Dower also pulled out of the returning formation in this aircraft when he decided he needed to throttle back to save fuel, accompanied by a wingman flying A-20G #42-86615. Dower previously radioed squadron commander Richard Walker requesting the formation reduce speed but Walker refused, fearing that slowing down was more dangerous than fuel consumption. They became temporarily lost but found the coast by which time they were both critically short of fuel. Dower put down at Yamai airfield but the airframe was written off. It was later salvaged for parts by a service squadron.

2. A-20G serial 43-9401 672nd BS/417th BG

Forced-landed at Yamai strip by Lieutenant Phillip Crow and written off. Fuselage salvaged for parts by the RAAF in 1985.

3. A-20G serial 43-9629 675th BS/417th BG, tail letter E

Flown by Lieutenant Edward Davidson, this aircraft's left-hand main gear collapsed while landing in mud at Yamai strip. The crew suffered minor injuries, but the aircraft was written off. Afterwards, all crews which put down at Yamai were transported by USN barge to Saidor arriving at 2100. The airframe was salvaged by the RAAF in 1985.

4. A-20G serial 43-9491 13th BS/3rd BG

This bomber was written off by an unidentified pilot at Yamai. The fuselage was salvaged by the RAAF for parts in 1985.

5. A-20G serial 42-86615 13th BS/3rd BG, tail letter T

Forced-landed at Yamai by unidentified Donald Dower's wingman (see account in Loss 1 above), this aircraft was written off after the undercarriage collapsed and twisted its fuselage. The airframe was salvaged by the RAAF in 1985.

6. A-20G serial 43-9186 13th BS/3rd BG, tail letter E, *Honeybunch*

Honeybunch's main gear collapsed when landing through aircraft wreckage at Saidor. It was subsequently repaired.

7. A-20G serial 43-9399 675th BS/417th BG, tail letter N

Lieutenant Duane Aamodt's right wing impacted with an unidentified B-25D while landing at Saidor. Both aircraft were later repaired.

8. A-20G serial 42-86768 90th BS/3rd BG

Borrowed from the 90th BS, this bomber was belly-landed at Saidor by an unidentified pilot, as it came to rest it struck *Dirty Old Man*, a 348th FG P-47D. The A-20G was later repaired and assigned to the 90th BS where it was named *Barry's Baby*.

9. A-20G serial 42-86713 13th BS/3rd BG, tail Letter W, *Powerful Katrinka*

This aircraft led the 13th BS and was flown by Major Richard Walker, with navigator Lieutenant Donald Lees also aboard. As Walker landed in the confusion at Saidor his wingman Lieutenant Linzemier flew underneath him and interrupted his approach. *Powerful Katrinka* skidded off the side of the runway shoulder and came to rest alongside a mud embankment after its nosewheel collapsed. It was later repaired and transferred to the 90th BS, the 8th BS and then finally to the CRTC in November 1944.

10. A-20G serial 42-86772 387th BS/312th BG, tail Letter J, *Benny's Baby*

Lieutenant Glen Benskin put *Benny's Baby* down in a swamp northeast of Annenberg with its gear retracted. Several rescue attempts saw Benskin and his gunner "JJ" Westerman eventually flown to safety in a 25th Liaison Squadron L-5A. Parts of the airframe were salvaged by RAAF in 1985.

11. A-20G serial 42-86786 388th BS/312th BG, tail Letter F, *The Hell'n Pelican II*

This bomber flown by Lieutenant Charles Davidson with gunner Sergeant John McKenna forced-landed gear-up near Amaimon village at 1715. Both crew were subsequently collected by the RAN store carrier HMAS *Matafele* on 1 May 1944 in Madang harbour after the crew had floated down the Gogol River. It was salvaged by the RAAF in 1984 for static restoration which was completed in April 1996. At time of publication the aircraft was on display at the RAAF Amberley Aviation Heritage Centre.

12. A-20G serial 43-9039 13th BS/3rd BG, tail Letter S, *Joy Baby*

Joy Baby (with the name *Jane* on the lefthand cowl) was flown by Lieutenant Billy Sanders and forced-landed on the coast gear-down near the mouth of the Malas River, not far from Tokain village. Both crew were rescued by VP-34 PBY-5 Blackcat #73 commanded by Lieutenant James Merritt the following day (official records state the crash location as "Tariltce"). At time of publication the wreckage still lay where it came to rest.

13. A-20G serial 43-9098 387th BS/312th BG, tail letter S, *The Texan*

The Texan was ditched by squadron commander Captain Frank Smart with gunner Sergeant Mike Music south-southeast of Bogadjim at 1735. Although both crew were seen in the bomber's dinghy immediately after ditching they were never found, and both were classified MIA in 1949. At time of publication the aircraft still lies on a sandy seabed.

14. A-20G serial 43-9488 675th BS/417th BG, tail letter V

One of nine 675th BS A-20Gs which diverted to Finschhafen, this aircraft was ditched by Lieutenant Michael Jovanovich some 35 miles northwest of Finschhafen at 1655. Jovanovich was rescued by a PT boat, but gunners Sergeants Jack Barr and Melvin Cope went down with the aircraft.

15. A-20G serial 43-9628 388th BS/312th BG, tail letter A, *Lady Constance*

Lieutenant Joseph Gibbons forced-landed this bomber near Wabusarik village. Both crew were rescued by a 25th Liaison Squadron L-5A nearly a week later. The RAAF salvaged parts of the aircraft in 1985.

16. A-20G serial 43-9669 672nd BS/417th BG *In The Mood*

Lieutenant Arthur Gresens landed at Saidor during the height of confusion. His A-20G drove through the burning wreckage of the mid-runway crash and came to rest against an embankment. None of the crew was injured but *In the Mood* was destroyed.

17. B-24D serial 42-72946 403rd BS/43rd BG *Here 'Tis*

Here Tis was flown by Lieutenant Raymond Cooley and went missing 50 miles north of the emergency field at Faita in the Ramu Valley. It was last seen climbing through thick cloud at approximately 1500. The crew of ten was subsequently classified MIA, however, in fact it crashed in formation about 700 metres apart from Loss 19 (B-24J 42-100225) at an altitude of 4,700 feet near the village of Kunukio in the Finesterre Ranges. The crash site was identified in 2001.

18. B-24J serial 42-109977 19th BS/22nd BG

Lieutenant RL Anderson swerved to avoid an oncoming Mitchell when landing at Saidor, collapsing this Liberator's undercarriage. It was later repaired.

19. B-24J serial 42-100225 408th BS/22nd BG tail Letter V

Captain Thomas Paschal and his crew were last sighted in formation 20 miles northeast of the coastal village of Bogadjim at 1450. The aircraft was subsequently classified MIA, however in fact it crashed in formation about 700 metres away from Loss 17 (B-24D # 42-72946) at an altitude of 4,700 feet near the village of Kunukio in the Finesterre Ranges. The crash site was identified in 2002.

20. B-24J serial 42-109975 408th BS/22nd BG (no tail letter)

Shortly after take-off from Nadzab, Lieutenant James Rayzor's Liberator crashed four miles northwest of Gusap airfield, killing seven crewmembers. About 25 minutes after departure Rayzor shut down three engines due to mechanical problems. Unable to remain airborne with one remaining engine, the bomber descended too steeply for a controlled landing, crashing about a mile short of Gusap's runway.

21. B-24J serial 42-110000 408th BS/22nd BG

Unsure of his position in thick cloud, Lieutenant Robert Stone ordered his crew to abandon the aircraft over mountains, 20 miles northeast of Bogadjim. Eight crewmembers survived but two remain MIA.

22. F-7A 42-73042 20th CMS/6th PRG

Lieutenant Royce Harms' reconnaissance Liberator was hit by flak in two engines over Hollandia. It was difficult to control when landing on Saidor's slippery, muddy surface where it slid left into a mud embankment and broke its back. The crew sustained no injuries, but the brand-new F-7A was scrapped for parts.

23. B-25D serial 41-30337 405th BS/38th BG

Lieutenant Robert Huhn's Mitchell collided head-on with Lightning F-5A #42-67350 in the smoke-reduced visibility of Saidor's runway. Both aircraft were destroyed, and their wreckage was bulldozed off the strip. Four crew, including Huhn, perished in the crash.

24. B-25D serial 41-30189 71st BS/38th BG *Sweet Jeanne*

Sweet Jeanne flown by Lieutenant Marshall Phillpit collided with B-25D *Seven Day Leave* (see Loss 25) during the landing roll at Saidor. It was later repaired by a service squadron.

25. B-25D serial 41-30611 71st BS/38th BG *Seven Day Leave*

This Mitchell flown by Lieutenant Paul Popma was impacted by Loss 24 at Saidor and was later repaired.

26. B-25G serial 42-64867 823rd BS/38th BG *Old War Horse*

Flown by Lieutenant Harvey, this Mitchell skidded sideways when landing at Saidor, collapsing its undercarriage. It was later repaired.

27. B-25D serial 41-30020 499th BS/345th BG *Stingeroo*

Flown by Lieutenant James MacWilliam, this strafer was ditched east of Kar Kar Island after low oil pressure caused an engine failure. After spending the night in their dinghy, the crew was rescued by a VP-34 PBY-5 Blackcat the next day, piloted by Lieutenant James Merritt

28. B-25D serial 41-30315 500th BS/345th BG *Tinkie*

This bomber was flown by Lieutenant James Waggle and was last seen at low altitude in formation near Bogadjim. It has never been located, and likely crashed into the sea.

29. B-25D serial 41-30527 823rd BS/38th BG *Fer-De-Lance*

Recently transferred from the 22nd BG, this Mitchell was forced-landed by Lieutenant Victor Maturi at Yamai. Its undercarriage collapsed and destroyed the airframe. At the time of publication, the airframe still lay where it came to rest.

30. F-5A serial 42-67350 26th PRS/6th PRG

Lieutenant Donald Christians' reconnaissance Lightning collided head-on with Loss 23 in poor visibility while landing at Saidor. Both aircraft were destroyed, and the flaming wreckage was immediately bulldozed from the runway to allow other aircraft to land. Christians was killed instantly in the crash.

31. P-38H serial 42-66668 36th FS/8th FG squadron #22 (previously *Corky Jr* with the 80th FS)

Lieutenant Robert Keown was seen circling off Yamai strip in poor visibility before he disappeared from view. Keown tried to climb over the Finisterre Mountains to return to Nadzab but baled out of the fighter in heavy weather shortly after leaving Yamai. It appears he was incapacitated by the fall as in the 1980s a villager located his remains in a swampy area and buried them in his village cemetery. The remains were handed over to a US recovery team in 1999, then in 2005 the wreckage of his P-38J was located by another villager. On 13 December 2017 the US military announced that the remains were Keown's.

32. P-38J serial 42-104352 433rd FS/475th FG squadron #182 (unnamed)

Lieutenant Joe Price landed this Lightning gear-up at Saidor following a narrow head-on runway collision with a B-25. The fighter came to a stop against an embankment.

33. P-38J serial 42-104310 433rd FS/475th FG squadron #175

Lieutenant Stanley Northrup's Lightning suffered a nosewheel collapse at Saidor when he successfully avoided a collision with a B-24. Both propellers were bent, however, the aircraft was later repaired.

34. P-38H serial 42-66832 80th FS/8th FG squadron #3

Lieutenant Lawrence Reeves was last seen circling off Yamai strip in a P-38H borrowed from the 80th FS. It is presumed that he crashed into the sea, and he remains MIA.

35. P-38H serial 42-66571 36th FS/8th FG

Lieutenant Eugene Zielinski baled out at 800 feet off Yalu Point near Yamai. He was rescued by a USN barge. His Lightning dove into the sea.

36. P-38J serial 42-104015 433rd FS/475th FG squadron #177

Lieutenant Robert Tomberg baled out near Bogadjim and returned to duty on 23 April 1944 after being guided to safety by natives. The crumpled wreckage of this fighter still lies on the jungle floor in the mountains behind Bogadjim.

37. P-38J serial 42-104351 433rd FS/475th FG

Lieutenant Calvin Wire's starboard engine clipped a tree whilst returning low along the coast, and he feathered its propeller. He flew into the ocean just off Yamai while attempting a second approach on one engine. He successfully kicked out of the cockpit and got into his dinghy which was blown towards shore where he was rescued shortly afterwards by two US soldiers in a canoe.

38. P-38J serial 42-104355 431st FS/475th FG

Lieutenant Milton MacDonald's Lightning was last seen in low cloud near Annenberg. The aircraft's wreckage was located post-war behind Madang near Efu village. MacDonald baled out not far from the village of Efu, and was captured and brought to Amron later that same afternoon, along with Lieutenant Austin Neely. Next afternoon both POWs were executed by sword. Amron was a Japanese hilltop outpost behind the former Japanese airfield at Alexishafen.

39. P-38J serial 42-104385 433rd FS/475th FG

Lieutenant Austin Neely was flying one of the trio of 433rd FS Lightnings last seen five miles west of the coastal village of Bogadjim in thick cloud. The wreckage of Neely's Lighting lies near the village of Amron. After baling out he was detained by a party of Japanese-appointed native policemen. Next afternoon he and Lieutenant Milton MacDonald were executed by sword.

40. P-38J serial 42-104390 433rd FS/475th FG squadron #185

Lieutenant Louis Longman was flying one of the trio of 433rd FS Lightnings last seen five miles west of the coastal village of Bogadjim in thick cloud. In fact, his fighter drove at high speed into the western end of the Finesterre Mountains near Shaggy Ridge Gap. Longman was 26 years old from Murdock, Minnesota.

41. P-38J serial 42-104381 433rd FS/475th FG

Lieutenant Lewis Yarbrough was flying one of the three 433rd FS Lightnings last seen five miles west of the coastal village of Bogadjim in thick cloud. In fact, this P-38J crashed and burned near the mountain village of Meibu, high in the Finesterres. In 2010 a US recovery team visited the crash site with investigations ongoing.

42. P-38J serial 42-67594 432nd FS/475th FG

Lieutenant Robert Hubner was last seen in formation with Lieutenant Jack Luddington. Hubner was last heard giving a distress call indicating his position as 60 miles southwest of Madang. Both Hubner and his Lightning remain MIA.

43. P-38J serial 42-67605 432nd FS/475th FG

Lieutenant Jack Luddington was last seen in formation with Lieutenant Robert Hubner and became MIA. Luddington's service dog tag was discovered on the corpse of a Japanese infantryman near the village of Afua in 1944, while the crumpled remains of his Lightning were discovered in 1948 behind Madang. Luddington's fate is recorded in a Japanese-language diary published in 2003 with excerpts from an unidentified Japanese intelligence solider, then based near the village of Aruso in the Madang district. The Japanese first met Luddington on 18 April 1944, two days after he baled out, with his parachute and bag holding water, food, emergency medical kit and a flare gun. When the Japanese decided to evacuate Madang they headed for Wewak, with POW Luddington entrusted to the Japanese diarist, even sharing the same mosquito net. The two became friendly during the retreat although Luddington was interrogated daily. Later he showed his girlfriend's photo kept in a pendant around his neck, and another of his family shelved in his notebook. The diarist recorded surprise that the US pilot's pistol appeared old-fashioned and heavy. Luddington was executed on the evening of 31 May 1944. By that stage the Japanese party was well west of Wewak and could no longer sustain the pilot who was in weakened health. Luddington was killed by sword, and his body was thrown into a river. His dog tag was retained as a souvenir.

44. P-38H serial 42-66555 36th FS/8th FG

Lieutenant Walter Mikucky became disorientated in overcast and spun in from low altitude, offshore from Yamai strip. He was presumed killed instantly and his body was not recovered.

45. P-39Q or N (serial unknown) 110th TRS/71st TRG

This aircraft was bellied-in by an unidentified pilot when landing at Saidor, and later repaired.

46. P-47D (serial unknown) 342nd FS/348th FG *Dirty Old Man*

This Thunderbolt was impacted by landing A-20G # 42-86768 while parked on the side of Saidor strip. It was later repaired.

APPENDIX 4

AIRCRAFT PROFILES

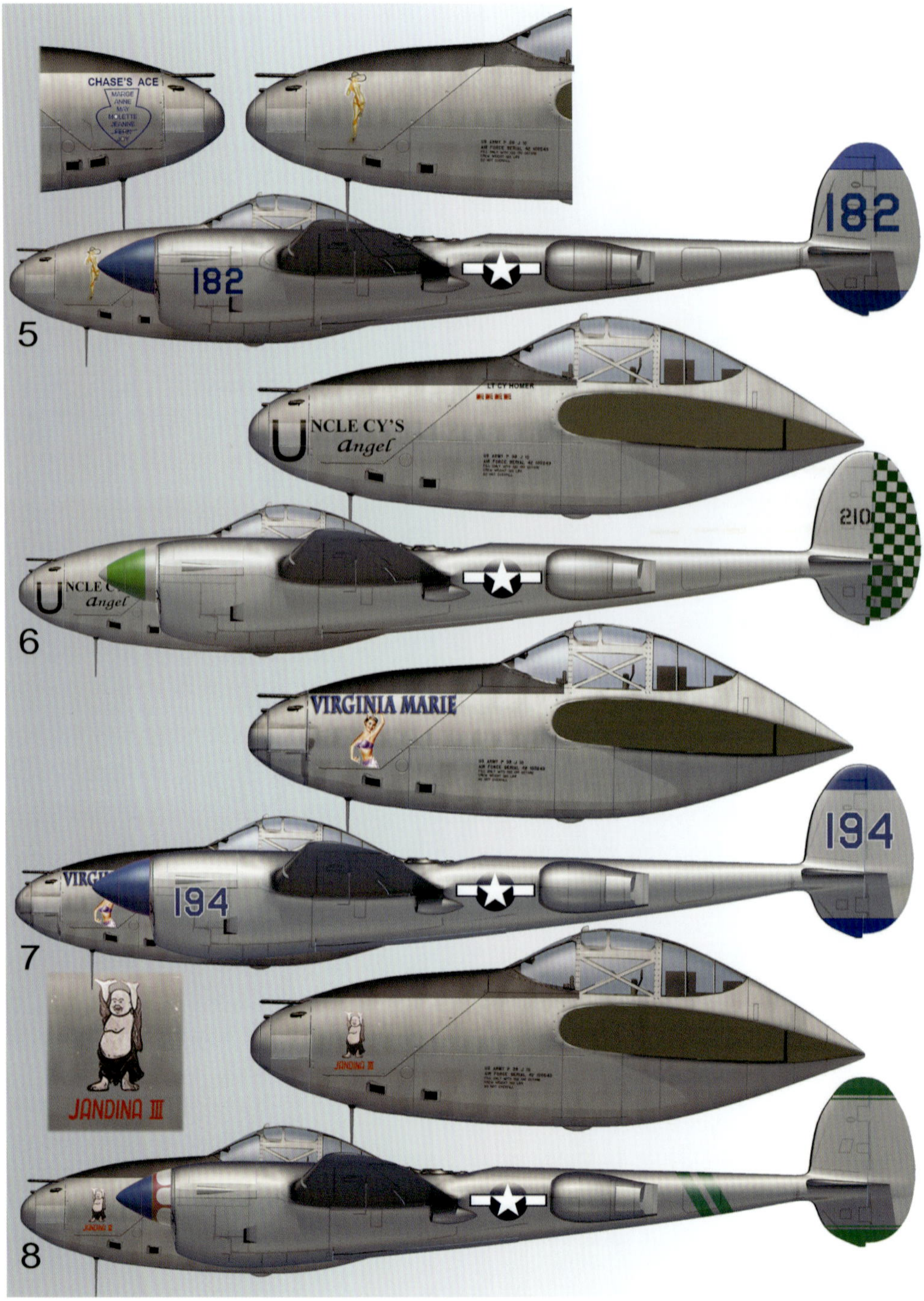
CHASE'S ACE
182
5
UNCLE CY'S
Angel
210
6
VIRGINIA MARIE
194
7
JANDINA III
8

FER-DE-LANCE
130527
9
Old War Horse
24367
10
THE BEAST
130606
11
'SWEET JEANNE'
130189
12
SEVEN DAY LEAVE
130611
13

THE EAGER BEAVER
130078

14

130315

15

PANNELL JOB
130024

16

53
227902

17

222929
74

18

CALIFORNIA
Sunshine
M
286776

19

PILOT CAPT F P Smart
CC SGT C S Sidek
ASST CC SGT D M Cooper
THE TEXAN
S
39098

20

PILOT-MAJ WELLS
Libby
W
321979

21

F
286786
THE HELL'N
PELICAN
II

22

POWERFUL
KATRINKA
W
286713
23
X
39501
HEKE'S
HOWE
24
HONEYBUNCH
E
39186
25
"MILK-EAR
WILLY"
L
39434
26

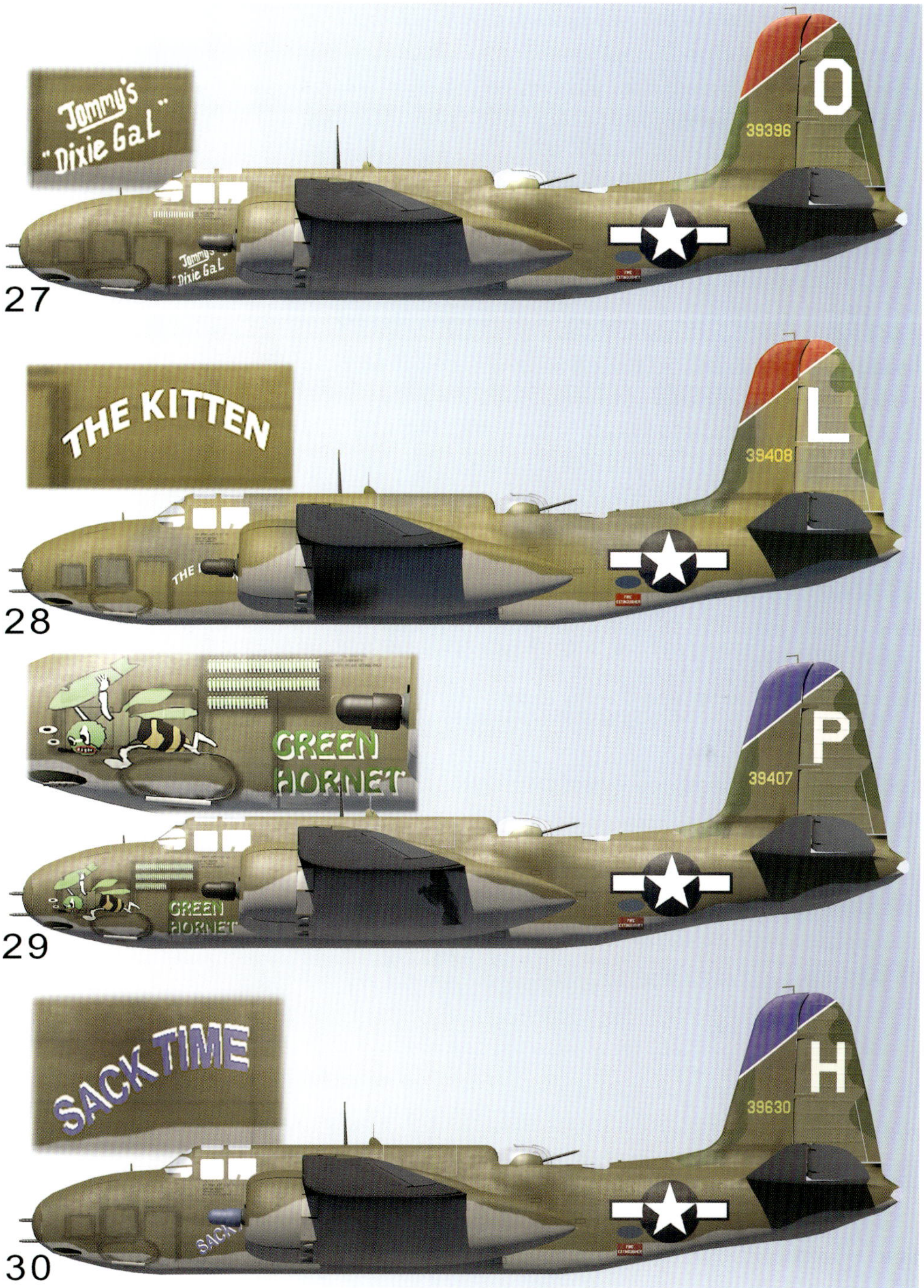
Tommy's "Dixie Gal"
O
39396
27
THE KITTEN
L
39408
28
GREEN HORNET
P
39407
29
SACK TIME
H
39630
30

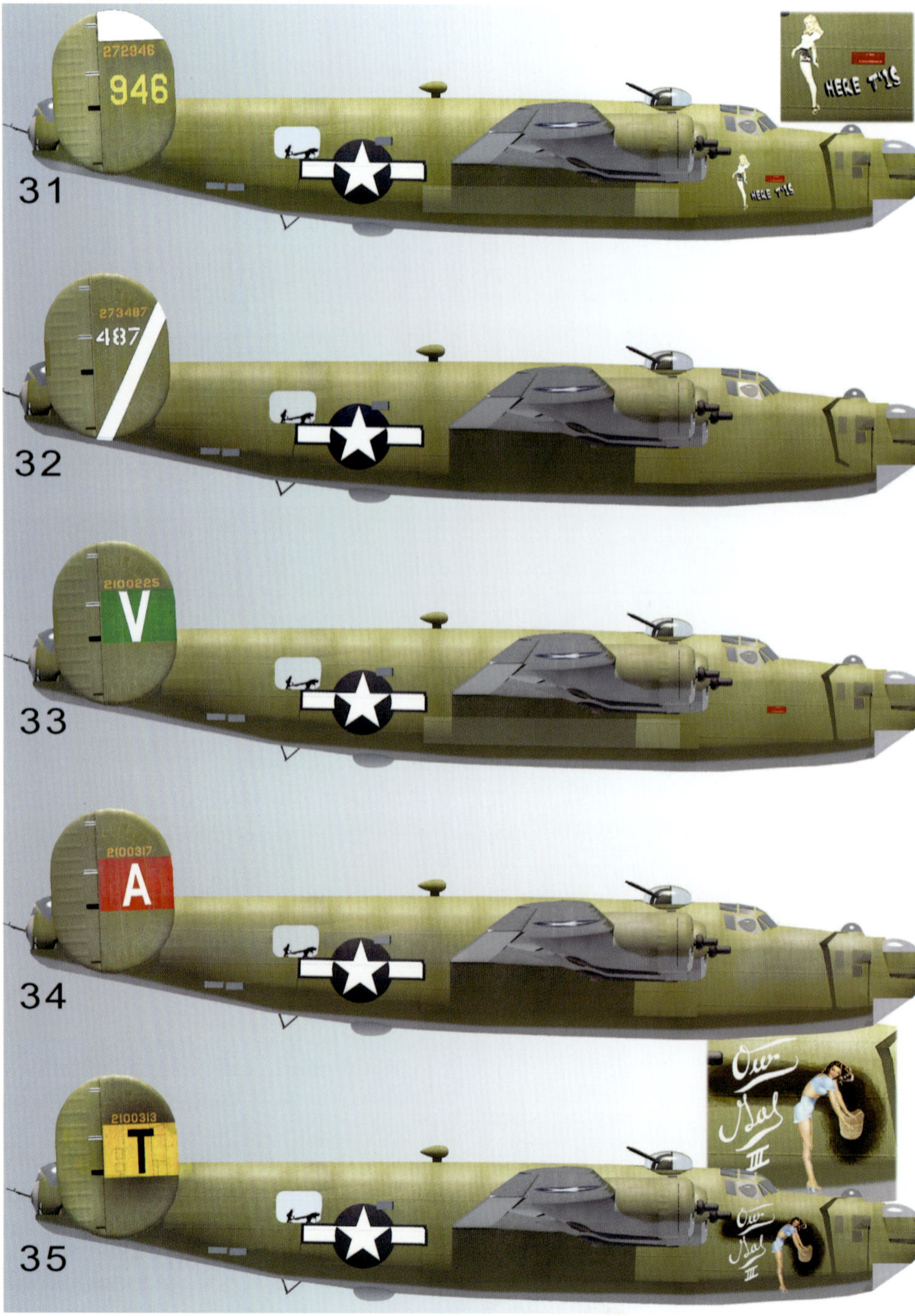
31
272946
946
HERE T'IS
32
273487
487
33
2100225
V
34
2100317
A
35
2100313
T
Our Gal III

273042
36
RBON
BOXCAR
273048
37
hangover
haven
264053
38
241216
HEAVEN CAN WAIT
39
KAY-O
263990
40

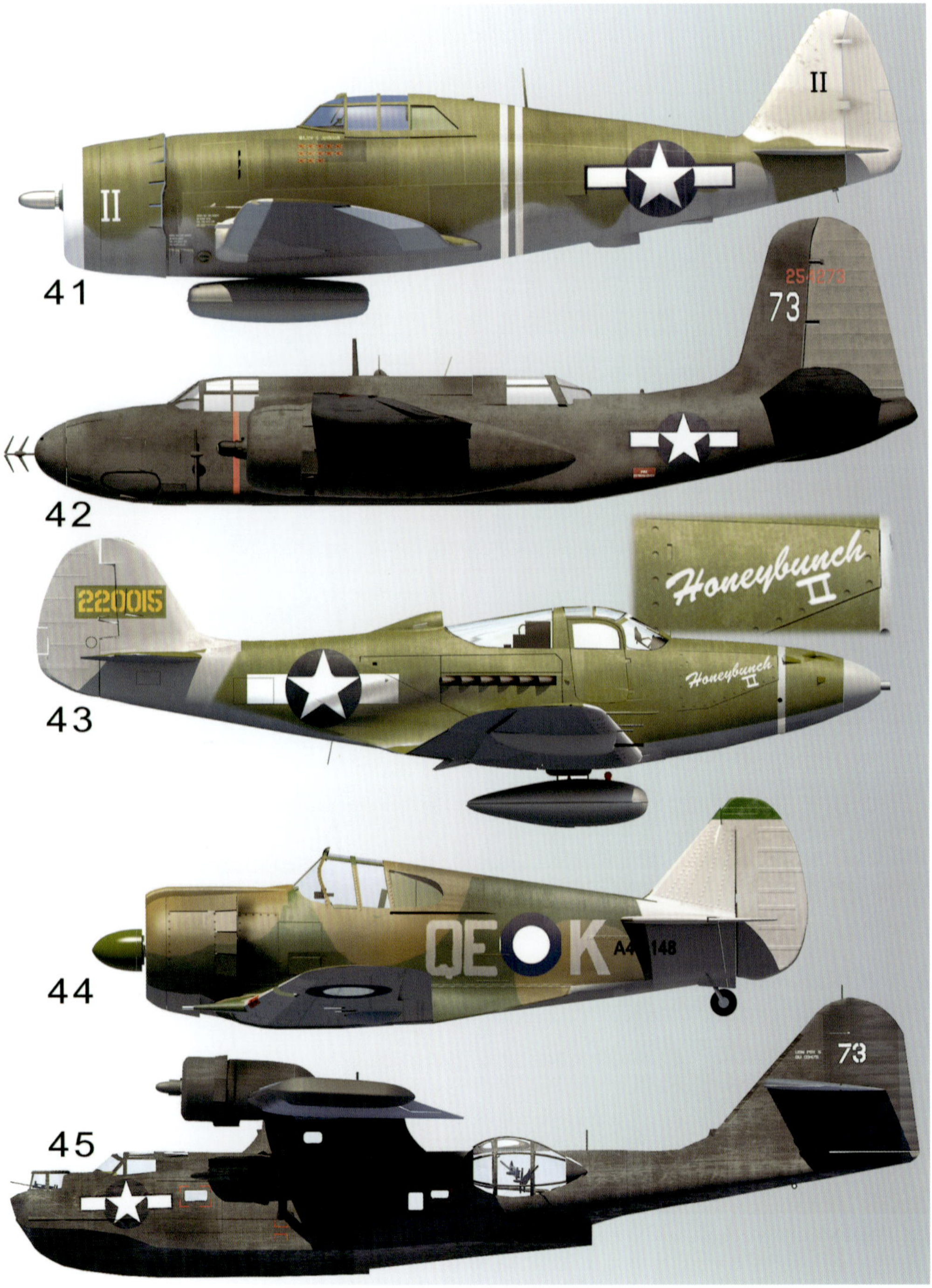
41
II
II
42
25-4273
73
43
220015
Honeybunch II
Honeybunch II
44
QE
K
45
73

Profile 1 – P-38J serial 42-104015 433rd FS/475th FG, squadron #177

Lieutenant Robert Tomberg safely baled out of this J model Lightning near Bogadjim. The fighter had been in the squadron inventory for a few weeks and retained the black serial on the fin. The squadron number was applied only to the outer cowls.

Profile 2 – P-38H serial 42-66668 36th FS/8th FG, squadron #22

Lieutenant Robert Keown went MIA in this P-38H when he climbed over the Finisterre Mountains to return to Nadzab but baled out instead. The fighter was one of several handed down to the 36th FS from the 80th FS where it was previously named *Corky Jr* and assigned to Major "Corky" Smith. The original nose art was painted over, and the aircraft was renumbered 22 on the nose and outer booms. Note that the stencilled Constructor's Number 1331 remained visible. The spinners were painted yellow the squadron colour.

Profile 3 – P-38J serial 42-104310 433rd FS/475th FG, squadron #175

Lieutenant Stanley Northrup flew this new J-15 model Lightning when he successfully avoided a landing collision with a B-24 at Saidor. The squadron number 175 was applied to the nose and the rear spinner was half painted blue.

Profile 4 – P-38J serial 42-67787 432nd FS/475th FG, squadron #169, *Marie Elena*

This fighter was one of several Olive Drab P-38J-10s delivered to Dobodura in late 1943, and was flown by Lieutenant William Elliot on the mission. All J models received by the 432nd FS after this batch were natural metal.

Profile 5 – P-38J serial 42-104494 433rd FS/475th FG squadron #182, *Chase's Ace*

This Lightning was the mount of Lieutenant Chase Breznier. The upside-down heart motif on the starboard gondola had seven female names representing wives and girlfriends of Breznier and his groundcrew. The name *Fern* was crossed out after one of them received a "Dear John" letter. This fighter flew on the mission with an unidentified pilot.

Profile 6 – P-38J-15 (serial unknown) 80th FS/8th FG, squadron Letter U, *Uncle Cy's Angel*

Uncle Cy's Angel was assigned to Lieutenant Cy Homer who flew the aircraft on the mission. Homer flew the 3 April 1944 Hollandia raid from which he claimed four kills, explaining the four kill markers. Homer later became squadron commander on 4 October 1944. Note the chequered green rudder which was featured on several 80th FS P-38Js at the time.

Profile 7 – P-38J-15 serial 42-104308 433rd FS/475th FG, squadron 194, *Virginia Marie*

Lieutenant Carroll Anderson received and named this fighter at Nadzab at the beginning of April 1944. He flew it on several Hollandia missions including Black Sunday.

Profile 8 – P-38J-15 serial 42-103988 80th FS/8th FG, *Jandina III*

The commander of the 80th FS, Captain Jay Robbins, received this fighter at Nadzab at the beginning of April 1944, replacing his previous J model with this one. All of Robbins' Lightnings carried an almost identical motif of the sumo wrestler. Robbins flew this fighter on several Hollandia missions including Black Sunday.

Profile 9 – B-25D serial 41-30527 823rd BS/38th BG, *Fer-De-Lance*

Lieutenant Victor Maturi put down this B-25 at Yamai, collapsing the undercarriage and destroying the airframe. The dark square at the top of both fins was where the previous 2nd BS logo was painted over.

Profile 10 – B-25G serial 42-4367 823rd BS/38th BG, *Old War Horse*

This Mitchell skidded sideways when landing at Saidor, collapsing its undercarriage. It was later repaired.

Profile 11 – B-25D serial 41-30606 822nd BS/38th BG, *The Beast*

This Mitchell had recently been transferred into the 822nd BS from the 408th BS which named it. It performed as the squadron photo-ship on the Black Sunday mission.

Profile 12 – B-25D serial 41-30189 71st BS/38th BG, *Sweet Jeanne*

Sweet Jeanne led the second flight of 71st BS Mitchells flown by Lieutenant Marshall Phillpit. It collided with Profile 13 during the landing roll at Saidor, but was later repaired by a service squadron.

Profile 13 – B-25D serial 41-30611 71st BS/38th BG, *Seven Day Leave*

This Mitchell was flown by Lieutenant Paul Popma and was impacted by Profile 12 at Saidor. It was later repaired.

Profile 14 – B-25D serial 41-30078 501st BS/345th BG, *The Eager Beaver*

This Mitchell was one of the nine 501st BS bombers which departed Nadzab to bomb Hollandia from medium altitude.

Profile 15 – B-25D serial 41-30315 500th BS/345th BG, *Tinkie*

Lieutenant James Waggle was last seen at low altitude in formation near Bogadjim flying *Tinkie*. It remains missing and likely crashed into the sea.

Profile 16 – B-25D serial 41-30024 500th BS/345th BG, *Pannell Job*

Pannell Job aborted the mission after reaching Burui with fuel transfer problems. It retains yellow cowls from its time with the 498th BS from which it was transferred on 8 April.

Profile 17 – P-47D serial 42-27902 40th FS/35th FG, squadron #53

This Thunderbolt was one of the sixteen from the 40th FS which set out from Gusap to escort B-25s bombers home. However, the entire squadron aborted due to the weather.

Profile 18 – P-47D serial 42-22929 41st FS/35th FG, squadron #74

This Thunderbolt was one of the sixteen 41st FS Thunderbolts which departed Gusap to escort A-20Gs home. However, the entire squadron aborted due to the weather.

Profile 19 – A-20G serial 42-86776 388th BS/312th BG, *California Sunshine*

The 388th BS commander Major Bill Kemble led the squadron from this bomber. The nose-art replicates the painting *Caught in the Draft* by US artist Gil Elvgren widely published in October 1943 calendars.

Profile 20 – A-20G serial 43-9098, 387th BS/312th BG, *The Texan*

This bomber was assigned from the 673rd BS and named by the 387th BS commander, Captain Frank Smart, in honour of his home state. He chose the tail letter "S" for his surname, and the white fin horizontal band 312th Bombardment Group marker was applied a few days before the mission. The dark oblique fin slant is where the previous 673rd BS marking was painted over. Smart and his gunner remain MIA after they ditched.

Profile 21 – A-20G serial 43-21979 389th BS/312th BG, *Libby*

The 389th BS commander Major Selmon Wells led the squadron on the mission from this bomber named *Libby* after his wife. The "W" on the rudder represented Well's surname, and the unique style of calligraphy was applied by squadron artist Sergeant Joe DiLorenzo only a few days before the mission.

Profiles 22 – A-20G serial 42-86786 388th BS/312th BG, *The Hell'N Pelican II*

This bomber was reassigned as *Gloria II* from the 3rd BG to Lieutenant Charles Davidson on 27 March 1944. Davidson forced-landed the bomber behind Madang. The aircraft was located by the author in 1976 and salvaged by the RAAF in 1984. It remains on static display at the RAAF Amberley Aviation Heritage Centre, Australia.

Profiles 23 – A-20G serial 42-86713 13th BS/3rd BG, *Powerful Katrinka*

Major Richard Walker flew this assigned A-20G on the mission, also photographing the road connecting Hollandia's airfields with nearby port facilities. *Powerful Katrinka* was field modified with an additional seat installed behind the pilot to carry a navigator. Lieutenant Donald Lees, the squadron's most experienced navigator, fulfilled the role on the mission.

Profile 24 – A-20G serial 43-9501, 8th BS/3rd BG, *Here's Howe*

This aircraft was assigned to Major Charles "Chuck" Howe as the 8th BS commander. Howe led the combined A-20G and B-25 contingent to the target from this bomber but overshot the target in doing so.

Profiles 25 – A-20G serial 43-9186 13th BS/3rd BG, *Honeybunch*

Honeybunch collapsed its maingear as it drove through Saidor's runway debris when landing.

Profiles 26 – A-20G serial 43-9434 89th BS/3rd BG, *Milk Ear Willie*

Lieutenant Charles Anderson who is caricatured in the nose art, flew this bomber profiled as it appeared a few days after the mission. The bomber barely made it back to Dumpu through the front. The next day Anderson proceeded to Nadzab where his crew chief declared his tanks almost empty. Technical Orders for this particular model A-20G specify it could board 730 gallons of fuel, but at Nadzab it boarded 734 gallons. Consequently, Anderson later painted and labelled a red circle with "100 Octane 734 gallons" under his caricature, as profiled here.

Profile 27 – A-20G serial 43-9396, 672nd BS/417th BG, *Tommy's Dixie Gal*

The 672nd BS operations officer Captain Edmund Fowler named his assigned aircraft in honour of a friend killed in the European theatre, Lieutenant Thomas Laird.

Profile 28 – A-20G serial 43-9408 672nd BS/417th BG, *The Kitten*

Although this bomber was named and mainly flown by Lieutenant Robert Kunselman, it was flown by another unidentified pilot on the Black Sunday mission.

Profile 29 – A-20G serial 43-9407 675th BS/417th BG, *The Green Hornet*

This A-20G served a month with the 388th BS before it was assigned to 675th BS operations officer Captain John Pryor on 10 April 1944. It was flown by Lieutenant George Young on the Black Sunday mission.

Profile 30 – A-20G serial 43-9630 675th BS/417th BG, *Sack Time*

Named by Lieutenant Albert Brokamp, this bomber was flown by Lieutenant Roy Andermann on the Black Sunday mission.

Profile 31 – B-24D serial 42-72946 403rd BS/43rd BG, *Here 'Tis*

This Liberator went MIA on the mission but crashed into the Finesterre range at 4,700 feet.

Profile 32 – B-24D serial 42-73487 65th BS/43rd BG

This profile showcases the tail markings of the 65th BS at the time of the Black Sunday mission.

Profile 33 – B-24J serial 42-100225 408th BS/22nd BG, tail letter V

This Liberator went MIA on the mission but crashed into the Finesterre range at 4,700 feet, not far from Profile 31 above.

Profile 34 – B-24J serial 42-100317 2nd BS/22nd BG, tail letter A

This profile showcases the red square tail marking of the 2nd BS. Flown by Captain Robert Brittain on the mission, the bomber was later named *Pleasure Bent*.

Profile 35 – B-24J serial 42-100313 33rd BS/22nd BG, tail letter T, *Our Gal III*

Our Gal III was flown by Lieutenant Louis Perraud on Black Sunday.

Profile 36 – F-7A serial 42-73042 20th CMS

Lieutenant Royce Harms' unnamed Liberator which was damaged during the landing roll at Saidor.

Profile 37 – F-7A serial 42-73048 20th CMS, *Bourbon Boxcar*

This reconnaissance Liberator wore a nose art masterpiece painted by artist Al Merkling. He started his artistic career by sketching tourists on Atlantic City's Boardwalk, and while his official role was that of lab technician, he spent most of his time on the flight line, armed with a paintbrush.

Profile 38 – F-7A serial 42-64053 20th CMS, *Hangover Haven*

Hangover Haven as it appeared on the Black Sunday mission before it was paint-stripped. On 22 April when flying this same aircraft Lieutenant John Noble could not find Madang in similar conditions to Black Sunday.

Profile 39 – B-24D serial 42-41216 320th BS/90th BG, *Heaven Can Wait*

This bomber was lost over Hansa Bay on 11 March 1944 during the lead-up to the Hollandia strikes and showcases the Jolly Rogers stencil applied to all the 90th BG's fins at the time.

Profile 40 – B-24D serial 42-63990 321st BS/90th BG, *Kay-O*

This Liberator led the 312st BS on the Black Sunday mission.

Profile 41 – P-47D (serial unknown), 9th FS/ 49th FG, squadron identifier II

The 9th FS commander Major Gerry Johnson flew this Thunderbolt from Gusap on Black Sunday to guide home stragglers. The white elevators indicated Johnson's leadership status, and the "II" tail marking indicates assignment to group headquarters. This Thunderbolt replaced Johnson's previous P-47D (squadron #83), which was transferred out in January 1944.

Profile 42 – P-70 serial 42-54273, 418th NFS, squadron #73

This P-70 was one two 418th NFS P-70s forward-deployed to Saidor on 1 April, and then used mainly for night patrols.

Profile 43 – Bell P-39Q serial 42-20015 82nd TRS, *Honeybunch II*

This Airacobra was assigned to 82nd TRS commander Major Donald Gordon who flew it from Saidor in April 1944.

Profile 44 – CAC Boomerang A46-148, RAAF No. 4 Squadron, squadron letters QE-K

This Boomerang was flown by Pilot Officer Keith Hindmarsh on the morning of Black Sunday for a reconnaissance searching for detachments of Japanese soldiers around Bogadjim. Over subsequent days it helped search for downed aircraft.

Profile 45 – Consolidated PBY-5 VP-34, squadron #73

This Blackcat was flown by Lieutenant James Merritt, USN, who rescued B-25D and A-20G crews on 17 April 1944.

SOURCES

Published Books

ALCORN, John S, The Jolly Rogers, Historical Aviation Album, Temple City CA 1981

BIRDSALL, Steve, Flying Buccaneers, New York, Doubleday 1977

CLARINGBOULD, Michael John, Helluva Pelican, Aerothentic Publications, Melbourne 1996

CLARINGBOULD, Michael John, The Forgotten Fifth, 1997

BLEAKLY, Jack, The Eavesdroppers, AGPS Publications, Canberra 1992

HEWITT, J.E, Adversity in Success, Langate Publishing, Melbourne 1980

KENNEY, George C, General Kenney Reports, New York, Sloan & Pearce 1949

KUPFERER, Anthony J, The Story of the 58th FG in WWII, Taylor Publishing, Dallas 1989

TOLL, Henry C, Tropic Lightning, Sunflower University Press, Kansas, 1987

YOSHINO, Ronald W, Lightning Strikes, Sunflower University Press, Kansas, 1988

Archive Material and Microfilm Records

Australian War Memorial & Australian Archives, Canberra, numerous files *inter alia*

Reconnaissance Binder 2/1/22

Ultra Intelligence Summaries/ misc/ March, April, May 1944

423-12-1 GHQ SWPA Situation Reports

48/302/64 Intercepted Enemy Traffic

ATIS - captured enemy documents, numerous

RAAF report: Survey of A-20 wrecks in Papua New Guinea 1984, Sqn Ldr Richard Lundbergh

Special Intelligence Bulletins HQ SWPA, General Staff MI Section

PNG Museum of Modern history, aircraft crash data index, via former curator, Bruce Hoy.

US Records

USAAF Memorandum EAR/SAP/1C672/10987 of 14 September 1949

VP-34 diary for April 1944

USAAF microfilm histories (Maxwell AFB), including Weekly Status and Operations Reports, Narrative Mission Reports, Unit Histories and MACRs, Escape and Unit histories and E&E reports for 2nd BS, 3rd BG, 5th Air Force, 8th FG, 8th BS, 13th BS, 20th CMS, 22nd BG, 25th Liaison Squadron, 26th CMS, 36th FS, 38th BG, 43rd BG, 80th FS, 89th BS, 90th BS, 90th BG, 110th TRS, 312th BG, 319th BS, 320th BS, 321st BS, 345th BG, 387th BS, 388th BS, (mission logs via Ralph Trout 1987), 389th BS, 408th BS, 417th BG, 431st FS, 432nd FS, 433rd FS, 475th FG, 499th BS, 500th BS, 501st BS, 672nd BS and 675th BS.

Missing Aircrew Combat Reports (MACRs)

4358, 4359, 4359, 4498, 4498, 4499, 4499, 4500, 4500, 4501, 4502, 4502, 4503, 4503, 4507, 5376 (all of 16 April 1944)

Letters/interviews/ diary extracts/ letters/ emails to author between 1979 and 2000 Unless otherwise indicated, all are/ were Fifth Air Force veterans.

Aiken, Ralph, 20th CMS, Amos, Bill, 22nd BG, Andermann, Roy 417th BG, Anderson, Carroll, 475th FG, Anderson, Lee, 312th BG, Atkinson, G. G, 58th FG, Auger, Elvin, 5th Air Force (1946), Bartlett, Walter, 312th BG, Benskin, Glen, 312th BG, Bistika, Ed, 312th BG, Bjorum, Carl, 421st NFS, Brown, Joseph, 3rd BG, Burgess, Dale, 432nd FS, Campbell, Donald, 8th FG, Clark, P.H, 43rd BG, Collins, John F, 405th BS, Colwell, Alfred B 38th BG, Commons, Samuel, 65th BS, Croft, Arthur F, 345th BG, Davidson, Charles, 312th BG, Devore, John 110th TRS, Down, Stewart, 312th BG, Erdmann, Orville, 8th FG, Ertzbischoff, George 417th BG, Esposito, Joseph, 43rd BG, Fairbanks, Dexter, 43rd BG, Fehrmann, Zane, 38th BG, Flannery, George, Fifth Bomber Command Headquarters, Gresens, Art, 672nd BS, Grills, Richard, 90th BG, Hanks, Robert, 43rd BG, Happ, Len, 312th BG, Harris, Virgil, 69th Service Squadron, Hatch, Asa, 22nd BG, Hellstrom, John, 22nd BG, Henebry, John, 3rd BG, Heyer, Walter, 89th BS, Heyman, Bertram, 312th BG, Hitchcock, Donald 345th BG, Holman, Richard, 342nd FS, Hoover, William, 5th Bomber Command, Howell, Lawnton, 38th BG, Hoy, Bruce, Curator PNG Museum, Jack, Jean A, Former Commander CRTC (Port Moresby), Johnson, Milton, 417th BG, Kemble, William 312th BG, Kimball, Elizabeth (Wife Of Richard), 475th FG, Kitchens, Ralph, 58th FG, Kobaly, Johnnie, 475th FG, Lord, Andrew, 90th BG, Mcclure, Otis, 20th CMS, Mcclurkin, J.R, 110th TRS, Monahan, Gus, 90th BG, Mullady, John, 33rd BS, Nichols, Paul, 43rd BG, Pavel, Lew, 38th BG, Pennefather, David, (former Papua New Guinea Patrol Officer), Perrin, Alex, Australian Infantry Spotter, Pettus, James, 43rd BG, Popma, Paul, 38th BG, Price, Joe, 475th FG, Purdy, Jack, 475th FG, Raaka, Douglas, 3rd BG, Radnik, Martin, 3rd BG, Rankin, Hobart 345th BG, Ransier, John, 3rd BG, Rieman, Clarence, Robbins, Jay, 20th CMS, Rogala, Ben 3rd BG, Ross, Leroy, 475th FG, Roth, Bob, 43rd BG, Shaltz Bob, 3rd BG, Shenton, Howard, 58th FG, Smith, Donald, 3rd BG, Smith, Robert 8th FG, 6 August 1994, Solomon, William, 43rd BG, Spence, Leslie, 3rd BG, Strauss, Robert, 312th BG, Stuart, Nelson, 90th BG, Sullivan, Roger, 43rd BG, Sweeney, James 22nd BG, Terrell, Harry, 38th BG, Toothman, Robert, Turner, Dwight 3rd BG, Turner, Noel 22nd BG, Turner, William, 8th FG, Walker, Richard, 13th BS, Wandrey, Ralph, 49th FG, Weigel, Andrew, 3rd BG, Wells, Challen, 20th CMS, Wells, Robert, 82nd TRS, Wells, Selmon, 312th BG, Welton, Allen 90th BG, Wire, Calvin, 475th FG, Woodall, Ben, 20th CMS, Woods, Wiley, 90th BG, Wulf, Lawrence, 22nd BG.

INDEX OF NAMES